Contents

PUTTING THEOLOGY

TO WORK

A THEOLOGICAL SYMPOSIUM

ON

Unemployment and
the Future of Work

Edited by

Malcolm Brown
and
Peter Sedgwick

CCBI, Inter-Church House   The William Temple Foundation
35-41 Lower Marsh   Manchester Business School
London SE1 7RL   Manchester M15 6PB

© 1998 The William Temple Foundation
Published by
CCBI, Inter-Church House, 35-41 Lower Marsh, London SE1 7RL
The William Temple Foundation, Manchester Business School,
Manchester M15 6PB

ISBN 0 85169 243 5 (CCBI)
ISBN 1 870 733 17 7 (WTF)

Printed by Tyndale Press (Lowestoft) Ltd.
Tyndale House, Wollaston Road, Lowestoft, Suffolk, NR32 2PD

Foreword

The report *Unemployment and the Future of Work: An Enquiry for the Churches* has been widely perceived as a landmark from the political, ecclesiological and theological perspectives.

In the social and political context of Britain in 1997, the publication of *Unemployment and the Future of Work* just before a General Election which saw a landslide victory for 'New Labour', has probably ensured that the report will gain a substantial reference in any comprehensive historical account of the age. It is far too soon, though, to judge whether the congruence of tone (though not of every aspect of policy) between the report and the new government will cause the report to endure as a seminal document or to be submerged beneath a new social orthodoxy which could hardly have been predicted prior to the election. The sincere affirmation of the report by the Chancellor, Gordon Brown, at the conference on *Unemployment and the Future of Work* in September 1997 and the response of the Archbishop of Canterbury were widely reported as ushering in a new era of church-state co-operation. Others present that day reflected that the test would come when the government's extended honeymoon with the electorate drew to an end and hard choices in an ethically plural society could not be fudged.

This theme of plurality versus consensus infuses not only the political debate, but that among theologians as well. That tension is reflected in this symposium. But it is worth noting that it was precisely the issue of seeking consensus within a plural context, which makes the report a landmark for the churches. For this was the first major issue that had been tackled by the churches together, through the structures of the Council of Churches for Britain and Ireland (CCBI) rather than by denominations acting alone. The national media generally failed to comprehend the ecumenical nature of the Enquiry, let alone the significance of the wide denominational ownership of the process. Nevertheless, one consequence of the report's reception is that it will now be very difficult for individual denominations to command a similar authority in the public domain when they tackle social and political controversy. Concern at prevailing unemployment and anxieties about the future of work contributed a common starting point for the Enquiry - a consensus about the problem within which diverse approaches to solutions and to methods could be debated. Even that degree of diversity was hard to handle, as Patrick Coldstream relates, so perhaps ecumenical ownership of social theology has yet to be tested to the full. Challenges remain about what can be attempted together and about the ways in which denominational energies and resources contribute to making ecumenical 'interfacing' with society a reality.

Underlying the questions of inter-church politics lies a concern for the development of a social theology that is enriched by diverse histories and traditions and which engages with developments in the confessional communities, and the academy. It is the purpose of this symposium to examine the extent to which the *Unemployment and the Future of Work* report represents a milestone, if not a landmark, in the development of an adequate social theology for today. The report was certainly innovative in the way it attempted to integrate sound theology with equally sound economics. Because it set out to address both the churches and the secular world it eschewed both the 'tacked on theological chapter' and the temptation to interpret its whole brief through the conceptual framework of the theologian. How far it succeeded is, of course, a matter for debate, and the contributors to the symposium are not of one mind on this. Nevertheless, it was always acknowledged that the report's authority would rest not only on its economic competence, but on its wide ownership within the churches - and this in turn would depend upon the theological content being recognised and (broadly) accepted within the churches.

So a Theological Consultation in July 1997 represented an early testing of the work of the Enquiry by members of one of the constituencies it had to address - professional theologians. The idea for the Consultation came from the Board for Social Responsibility of the Church of England and the event was co-ordinated by the William Temple Foundation, an ecumenical research and training body for the churches' work in economics and urban communities, based in Manchester Business School where the Consultation was held.

This symposium represents the work of that Consultation. It is not intended to be a 'Theology of Unemployment' or of 'work' - that is another task. Rather it is an exploration in theological method using the report as an exemplary case study. Nor is it intended as a final word but as an early contribution to a debate that will need to continue and which is of significance well beyond *Unemployment and the Future of Work*.

The thanks of the editors is due to all the contributors who presented papers to the Consultation, those who contributed reflections afterwards and to all the participants who made the event such a lively exchange of ideas. Our thanks are also due to Colin Davey at CCBI for assistance in bringing the papers to publication, and Linda Dunning of the William Temple Foundation for word-processing the text.

Malcolm Brown
October 1997

The Contributors

Patrick Coldstream CBE chaired the Working Party that conducted the Enquiry. He is Director of the Council for Industry and Higher Education.

Andrew Britton was Executive Secretary to the Churches' Enquiry on Unemployment and the Future of Work. He was formerly Director of the National Institute of Economic and Social Research.

The Rev'd Dr Peter Sedgwick is Assistant Secretary at the Board for Social Responsibility of the General Synod of the Church of England.

Professor Ian Markham is Liverpool Professor of Theology and Public Life at Liverpool Hope University College.

The Rev'd Malcolm Brown is Executive Secretary of The William Temple Foundation, Manchester.

The Rev'd Professor Ronald Preston is Professor Emeritus of Social and Pastoral Theology at the University of Manchester.

Dr Elaine Graham is Lecturer in Social and Pastoral Theology at the University of Manchester.

The Rev'd Professor Duncan Forrester is Dean of the Faculty of Divinity, Edinburgh University.

The Rev'd Dr Nigel Biggar is Chaplain and Fellow of Oriel College, Oxford

Introduction

Peter Sedgwick

The Report, *Unemployment and the Future of Work*, was published on April 8, 1997 during the General Election campaign. The Report was sponsored by the Council of Churches for Britain and Ireland, and sprang out of the concern which the Bishop of Liverpool, Bishop David Sheppard, had about unemployment in British society. His burning anger at the harm caused by unemployment, and his compassion for its victims, gradually persuaded others that the churches must face the issue head-on. It was not enough to say that unemployment was too technical and complex an issue to address.

Hence the Report came to be written. As I write this preface at the end of September 1997, the Report has been discussed from small parish meetings to national conferences addressed by the Chancellor of the Exchequer, who paid a heartfelt tribute to the churches in general, and Bishop Sheppard in particular, for bringing *'the concerns of unemployment to the centre of the political agenda.'* It was not the only report to have been written at this time by the churches, for the Roman Catholic Church in England and Wales produced *The Common Good*, whilst in Wales CYTUN (Churches Together in Wales) responded to John Redwood's challenge and wrote *Wales: A Moral Society? Unemployment and the Future of Work* was, however, the most substantial report, drawing on the first-hand experience of a working party which visited different regions in the United Kingdom and the Republic of Ireland.

The Report was published just as the long era of Conservative government was drawing to a close after eighteen years. The euphoria in many parts of Britain, which followed the election result, reflected a desire for change. This change was not simply political but cultural, and was shown in the public reaction to the death of Diana, Princess of Wales. It was shown too in the vote on Scottish devolution, and rather less clearly in the Welsh referendum. There was a feeling that it was time for a more inclusive, less hierarchical and stratified society, where people could express their own feelings and have their own culture recognised. Part of the curse of unemployment is the sense of powerlessness and constraint that it engenders in the heart of communities and individuals. Nor should we forget that the Report is also entitled *'and the Future of Work'*. Here again the mood of cultural change is caught clearly. Questions about the role of women and ethnic minorities in the labour process; part-time work

1

and early retirement; lifelong learning and high technology all impinge here. The Chair of the Working Party, Patrick Coldstream, has long had these concerns at the centre of his working life, while Andrew Britton as Secretary to the Working Party has analysed these changes with great skill in his former post as Director of the National Institute.

At this point, however, a cautionary note must be heard. So far the discussion has been about economics, cultural change and Christian compassion. Is this then a report which describes the condition of Britain in 1997, and asks for changes in that society because Christians must protest when the ungodly *'ravish the poor: when he getteth him into his net'* (Ps 10:10)? Or is the very analysis of Britain, and the rising desire for social and cultural change, which the Report itself embodies, dependent on a different language - the language of theology? And how might that language resonate with the cultural, social and economic analysis, which runs through the Report?

It was questions such as these which led to a consultation in Manchester in July 1997, arranged by The William Temple Foundation alongside The Church of England Board for Social Responsibility. Some twenty theologians, from places as diverse as Cardiff, Edinburgh, Oxford and London, heard Andrew Britton and Patrick Coldstream speak to the Report they had produced. They were followed by a number of presentations designed to draw out the different theological approaches that can be taken to the Report. It is these presentations, with some comments written after the day by some of the participants, which make up this book.

It is clear that theological work in Britain is in some turmoil. Both Ian Markham and Malcolm Brown draw attention to the criticisms made of the mainstream English tradition of social ethics from 1945 - 1990 by such writers as John Milbank, Oliver O'Donovan and Michael Banner. (Professor Banner had hoped to be present, but unfortunately had another engagement). The argument, as set out by Markham, is that there is now a powerful critique of English, liberal social ethics as insufficiently theological. Since the Report stands largely in that tradition, it falls under that stricture.

A similar point was made by another correspondent who, again was unable to attend the conference. In a letter about the Report and ideas of redistributive justice, he wrote that modern democracies have evolved ideas of justice that, for him, were *'based on prudential notions about social coherence'.* It seemed *'implausible... to dress them up as absolute principles with a theological foundation'.* Biblical ideas of justice were not to be subsumed under contemporary arguments for social order so lightly.

Both Markham and Brown set out their objections to the criticisms of the Report. As Brown says, *'theologians like Michael Banner and John Milbank are raising questions which demand answers and their analysis of the plural social condition is acute'.* Nevertheless dialogue is possible, even though the cultural change out of which the Report is written is not easy to handle. Plurality is a difficult condition for theology to respond to. There is pluralism within society, and within theology itself.

Markham refers to his own book, *Plurality and Christian Ethics,* and argues for a cultural and social ethic, which has a strong environmental emphasis, lacking in the Report itself. Brown appeals for an *'experimental practice',* which makes a virtue out of provisional alliances and shared encounters. It is a search for *'limited goals',* rather than a definitive position.

Ronald Preston is critical of the Report for not tackling two issues. One is once again what he calls *'a persistent Christian undercurrent which refuses to take Economics seriously'.* The second is the issue which ran through the General Election: should there be even less government interference in the economy than was the case at the end of 1997 Conservative government? Preston is less concerned with pluralism than with the political choices faced by Christians in their response to unemployment.

The two major presentations were by Elaine Graham and Duncan Forrester. Graham places the Report in the context of *Faith in the City,* the 1985 Anglican report on urban deprivation. Graham analyses the Unemployment report in some detail, and asks what kind of church does it presuppose? Again pluralism and social change become prominent, but seen this time through the communities of faith that contribute to different theologies. Graham feels that the Report misses *'an opportunity to reflect the complexity and richness of ecumenism'.* Despite good intentions, she finds the values of the Report rather disembodied and unspecific. Forrester writes from an interesting perspective. He is a Scottish Reformed theologian, but his visits to the United States have interested him in North American Catholic social ethics. This raises fears in Forrester's mind that both the American theologians, who rely heavily on a natural law framework, and the British report, are in danger of suppressing the voices of dissent, often without seeking to do this. There is much that Forrester likes about the Report, such as its move beyond middle axioms to specific policy recommendations. Nevertheless the Report is too cerebral for him: *'the general style of the Report swings between that of a Royal Commission, and that of a book of theology'*. Although there are good passages of theology in the Report, and his overall comment is that it *'is a distinguished contribution to public debate and to social theology'*, still it is insufficiently theological. An intriguing point follows: that the Report reflects the state of British social theology, and its lack of progress since *Faith in the City*. And that leads him to pleading *mea culpa*, and hoping that other theologians will join in this apology.

Finally there is the contribution of Nigel Biggar. Biggar wrote a critique of the Report in *'Third Way'*, *('timely, prophetic and economically respectable rebuttal of the spirit of the age ... but only uncertainly theological')*. His contribution, like Preston's, was written after the event.

It is perhaps the most severe analysis of the Report. Biggar argues that there is a fundamental distinction, which the Report has missed. *'Politically, economically and ethically (it) has much to commend it'*. It is the theology which is *'disappointing'*. Biggar feels that the references to the spiritual aspects of work and unemployment are inadequate. There is a necessity, he believes, for Christian reports to spell out that being made in God's image is not *'a quaint religious expression for certain qualities of human being that all decent liberal folk take entirely for granted'*. He argues that unless this is done, theology will be seen to be redundant, and the Christian churches should *'volunteer to go out of business'*. In brief, is the Report not an expression of humanist philosophy with a dressing of spirituality and Christian compassion?

In the brief, and condensed, few pages that follow this attack, Biggar sketches out the theological dimensions of creativity, responsibility, the image of God and the Sabbath. This is then related to overwork and unemployment. Overwork is seen to be driven *'by an anxious desire to secure a sort of ersatz-immortality through the future of our deeds'*. What is needed is a fully theological critique of secular culture. The Report calls on page 7 for *'a vital spiritual transformation'* in society so that increased taxes could be seen as a contribution to the common good. Biggar feels that the task is greater than that, for it must involve a call to material sacrifice. That in turn requires a special role for the churches '*in bringing about the necessary spiritual transformation*'. Yet here the Report is silent: its witness to God is marked by '*feebleness*', and its '*prophecy fails to penetrate deep enough beneath the surface of secularist culture*'. In fact Biggar finds the Report shows '*almost no sign*' of recommending a theological analysis to '*a sceptical public*'.

There is no agreement between Biggar, Graham, Forrester, Preston, Markham and Brown. The theological turmoil alluded to by many of them is reflected in the diversity of the papers themselves. This, in turn, raises a sharp question in one's mind. It is a simple, but profound, statement: 'How will the debate be carried on?'

The Report certainly contributes to the desire for social change and cultural renewal evident since the election on 1st May 1997. There seems a commitment by government and industry to return to as close to full employment as is possible. But how does theology speak in this mood of change? Is theology itself changing, some calling for a more Christian, others for a less cerebral approach? Must it recognise the diversity and provisionality of its language, or should it identify the political changes that are necessary to implement the Report's findings? Can it become more open to the social diversity of its congregations, some of whom are poor and excluded? This collection of papers shows that, while most Christians generally accepted the economic analysis of the Report, the theological framework was much less so. Will Hutton, Editor of *The Observer*, wrote recently that the Report was a bold thing to do, but '*the Church has got the capacity to be even braver. When it speaks it has tremendous authority still.*' The debate about how it should speak comes across vividly in these pages: some feel a lack of theology, others that it is directed in the wrong direction. Yet overall there is high praise for the Report, and a concern that the restatement of Christianity as public truth should be carried on vigorously.

A Report for the Churches

Patrick Coldstream

What is a Christian enquiry like? The answer in our case is that it was quite unlike a secular one. Its aims, described at its launch, were to produce a report which

- offered a theological exploration of the issues;

- analysed the various emerging trends and evaluated the policy options from a Christian standpoint; and

- could attract the general approbation of the churches and be of real service to both Church and Society.

The Working Party was fifteen men and women, lay and ordained, from all the major denominations in England, Wales, Scotland and Ireland, North and South. We met around a square of tables crammed in the central chancel-space between the choir-stalls in a South London church. We were responsible for presenting this report to a commissioning body of elders, at Bishop-level so to speak, also drawn from all the major churches. However, the contents and conclusions are those of the Working Party alone. The Enquiry is *for* the churches, not *by* them.

We floundered a bit with the demand for a 'theological approach', which was itself a rephrasing of the earlier, and even more daunting, 'theological framework'. Some members, Working Party people of high intelligence and wide experience of the world of affairs, said they found the theology 'completely beyond' them; others differed in how the Christian vision ought to be related to the world model offered by economics, or (for example) to the oppressive complexities of the benefit system. We were exercised as to whether we should produce a socio-economic analysis, with theological reflection confined to a separate chapter or, on the other hand, try to allow the Christianity to inform the argument all the way through. Those did not seem trivial matters: approaches to them reflected deep convictions about how faith relates to society's life, and anxieties about how the churches should address largely non-Christian, largely non-religious nations. They were not trivial for another reason - constructive discussion of our tasks and our future report were frustrated while we sought a resolution. Time seemed to be going fast and confidence sank. Deadlines threatened alarmingly.

I should like to draw out five elements in the method of proceeding with which we eventually found we could go forward. Those will, I hope, provide material for others' theological critique:

(1)   Theological thinking should inform the Report throughout. Nor should it confine itself to a 'middle axiom' level of generality; an attitude of infinite respect for individuals, for example, could make all the difference to the detailed administration of benefit systems or employment schemes.

So although we are sure that the churches have no special expertise to offer in the solution of economic problems, Christian discussion of (say) work for the unemployed nonetheless sounds different from secular. Here is an example from the Report.

> *Society faces a very difficult dilemma in dealing with those few people who really do not want to work ... In Christian teaching there is a duty to work as well as a right to work. It is wrong to expect the community to support you, when you could perfectly well support yourself.*

> *That is the easy point to make. The more difficult question is how society should treat its members who do not appear to accept this obligation. Christian teaching also urges us to be generous, patient and forgiving so that no-one is beyond the reach of our concern. ...*

Again, and for example, John Chrysostom appears in our discussion of the benefit system and Pharaoh and the Israelites in the Chapter on *Fair Pay and Conditions of Work.*

But although the influence of scripture, tradition and Christian experience should be felt throughout the argument, we also felt that the Group should make its own starting-point, its sources of illumination and energy, separately explicit. Finally it should make some reflection (at the end of its text) on its own experience of its own process. So in the Introduction the Report states our faith held in common and sets out a vision of the Kingdom (used by an earlier Church Committee on Economic Affairs) which we share:

That vision of a good, and particularly a fraternal, society inspires every section of our report. It provides us with a compass-bearing for change and an ultimate standard of comparison for our survey of the current working world and its failure.

We saw ourselves at work in the context of two thousand years of Christian thinking on these matters. Indeed we think that a long perspective can be a Christian strength in the debate. That tradition too should be set out, we believe, so we asked an expert (Peter Sedgwick) to write a brief history of it for us, which appears as the Report's first Annex. And finally in a 'concluding reflection' we touch very briefly on the Working Party's own experience of its eighteen months of existing, hearing evidence, and discussion:

To be a member of this enquiry has involved a constant movement back and forth between our inheritance of faith and our experience of the plight of the unemployed and the ill-treated.

(2) Secondly, rather than scouring our inheritance for principles and rules from which to deduce policies and remedies, we would instead draw on it for illumination, for imagination, for indications of attitude, and for insights into how things are and might be. Individual Working Party members might put forward an image, a story, or the words of a Christian teacher, with the implied question to the group: 'doesn't this give us a new angle on it?' or 'doesn't this re-inforce the approach we have been discussing?' or 'how might we learn from Simone Weil's thinking?' The discussion, our conclusions, or the drafting might change direction (or change colour, one might say) with such an intervention - or it might not. In a sense, that was the test of its appropriateness at just that point in the long history of Christian discussion.

Some of the 'narratives and images' of scriptures on which we particularly, and often deeply, drew are on pages 3 to 5 of the Report's Introduction. They influenced our attitudes to what we saw and heard, conditioned how we saw and listened, and gave a distinctive cast to our thinking.

Thus:

> *Christians go back to the biblical description of men and women as 'made in God's image'. This points to humanity's being endowed with a sacred and indestructible dignity and with stewardship of a world that God himself saw 'was good'. All humans have the potential for creativity, responsibility and love; none may ever be treated as disposable, menial or unwanted. That is to say, among other things, that the economy is there to serve human beings, not human beings to serve the economy.*

That helps us to keep the apparent imperatives of efficiency and effectiveness in proportion; it warns us to be vigilant with our definition of a healthy economy.

(3)   The group was invited to address its report not only to the Churches but also to the nation at large. It was important, then, to avoid technical language or insiders' thinking. That also led us to draw on scripture and tradition particularly for insights about humanity, and about man in society together, rather than for those more directly about God. So we say:

> *More specifically in describing and interpreting what we have learnt and proposing a way forward we draw on particular narratives and images of scripture. These uniquely illuminate human tendencies and human possibilities, offering warnings and suggesting fruitful avenues of change.*

In fact the 'narratives and images' offered as key examples of those that inspired us are seen to illustrate in particular:

- the dignity of men and women;
- the economy as one way we are enabled to serve each other;
- that God's love and man's worthwhileness are not 'performance-related';
- that humans are tempted to simple-mindedness and impoverished thinking by excessive veneration of single attractive notions – intellectual idolatry;
- that the natural economic tendency for the strong to grow stronger while the weak weaken, needs an arrangement to offset it;
- that citizens ought not to pursue economic advantage to the very

limit, but go about their affairs in a generous spirit;
- that only a just and caring society will achieve real and lasting prosperity; and
- that society is best seen as organic and its citizens as being members of a living body. We are members one of another.

As restated there, those 'messages' do not quite carry the full numinous charge that scripture offers us. We felt, however, that the examples we chose are accessible to, and might well inspire, people outside the church as well as inside.

(4)   A fourth feature of the Working Party's journey was its acceptance of strong personal feeling, as well as strenuous thinking, in our debates. I believe the Report gains conviction from this; certainly members wanted it to be a wake-up call to action, a 'prophetic' statement, which needed to spring from authentic commitment by members to what they were trying to say.

Inevitably, then, debates left members vulnerable to have aspects of their own faith challenged, and meant they had to go through some heightened and threatening sessions.   A quite surprising proportion of members approached the chairman privately for comfort at different stages of the enquiry, having been somewhat bruised or offended in our process, or fearful of having bruised or offended others.

Undoubtedly we learnt, and some of us were changed, by that. It is probably inseparable from earnest and committed Christian discourse. I believe this engaged theology must engage more than the mind - and so is more than an intellectual activity or an academic discipline. It thus has to be, ought to be, a risky enterprise; and it is precisely the mutual concern of *agape* that must keep fragile things from being badly damaged.

(5)   Finally, we relied, more than a lay and quite worldly chairman might have expected, on prayer, which framed each of our meetings. It is earnestness that I remember best, and the sense, as I felt it, that the frustrations of some rather shapeless issues, and the huge diversity of personal experience, denominational doctrine, intellectual approaches, and private vulnerability, could come into proportion as we consciously re-oriented ourselves towards the transcendent Other outside and beyond us. It was sobering, inspiriting and cheering - I doubt we'd have managed without it. Certainly it would have proved impossible without it to achieve the particular prize of unanimity.

11

My aim has been to describe a venture in purposeful Christian conversation by the Working Party with those we visited or who visited us, amongst ourselves, and now with Church Members, Church Leaders, opinion-formers and the world at large. Everyone contributed to the conversation, which was rich, and energetic. It is portrayed, if tidied up, in the Report, magnificently written for us by Andrew Britton.

Yet we are still novices at such conversation. Contributions are good but could be better with teaching. There are insights from other thinkers and there are new ways of thinking, which would make the conversation even more fruitful. It is here, I think, that a future enquiry could benefit from having an academic theologian as consultant to the group. (Though of course, we ourselves benefited by having several theologically trained people as members.) There was room (in our case) for additional outside academic theological expertise, as well as economic expertise, to be on offer. The task is, perhaps, to bring other voices to the table, which enquiry members might otherwise not hear. It is not to provide the answers, but to enrich the Report and help members to reflect well on the process they are engaged in.

A Distinctively Christian Report

Andrew Britton

In setting up this enquiry, the Sponsoring Group was very conscious that a great deal had already been written on the subject of unemployment and the future of work. As an economist I was especially aware of this background, having written quite a few papers on the subject myself. But the task that we were set as a working party was not just to write another report on this subject. We were asked to provide 'a theological exploration of the issues' and to 'evaluate the policy options from a Christian standpoint'. So this was to be a 'distinctively Christian' Report. We did not always find this an easy aim to achieve. In this chapter I shall seek to explain what the difficulties were and how we tried to overcome them.

We can no longer assume, in addressing the general public at large, a familiarity with Christian language and teaching. Much of the audience we wanted to reach would simply not understand what we meant if we referred to the Trinity or the Incarnation. If we had included a separate chapter in our Report on theology, many of our potential readers would have skipped over it or been alienated by it.

This is not just a problem of understanding. We were conscious of writing for an audience which was only partly Christian. It was a great opportunity to show the relevance of our faith to the problems of the world. We had to speak with the authority of the gospel, but we could not assume that its authority would be universally recognised or respected. In this respect the situation has changed, certainly since the time of William Temple, significantly even in the last ten or twenty years.

The second difficulty of writing a distinctively Christian Report was to choose between the many different models of Christian engagement with the world, put forward by different schools of theology. Different schools were represented within the working party itself. Should we be quoting from John Stott or from Ulrich Duchrow? It proved easier in practice to agree on our conclusions and then to agree on the arguments to be used in support of them.

Church members share a common allegiance to Christ, but many of them have other allegiances as well, which they do not hold in common. Some Christians are also socialists or liberals, concerned about civil rights, the protection of the environment or equal opportunities for women and men. We were asked to write a report which would 'attract the general approbation of the churches', which probably meant a report which did not simply reflect the particular value judgements of the working party members themselves. But where do you draw the line between what is a distinctively Christian view and what is perhaps the consequence of the Spirit of God at work in the secular culture? In practice debates about social issues amongst Christians often divide on very conventional lines between the political philosophies of the left and the right.

Finally, and most fundamentally, there are tensions within Christianity itself. In addressing issues of work and of employment, as elsewhere, a balance has to be struck between justice and compassion, between establishing rights and offering service, between the Old Covenant and the New. Even if the whole of our society consisted of dedicated and enthusiastic Christians these tensions would still be there. Christian comment on social issues has never been easy to write, and it never could be.

It is fundamental to our approach that Christianity should run right through the Report. It crops up in every chapter and in some rather surprising places. For example, on page 15 a discussion on the effects of new technology on employment leads into a discussion of human creativity and what it means to be made 'in the image of God'. Similarly, on page 24 the economics of market structure is interwoven with Christian reflection on 'ambition and greed'. In chapter 4, especially pages 77 to 79, we explore the relation between an economy based on gifts and an economy based on wages, using a variety of Biblical references. Again in chapter 7, which is about the special problems facing the long-term unemployed, a decisive voice is heard from the teaching of Jesus himself (p. 125). These are just a few examples to illustrate the point that the Report never allows economics and Christianity to lose contact with each other. Although many different kinds of argument are used in the Report, there is no compartmentalisation of Christianity out of touch with the secular disciplines.

As a Church Report, *Unemployment and the Future of Work* is unusual in addressing so many technical issues of economics - and in having a professional economist as its main author. This was necessary because one of its main tasks has been to counter the fatalism that says nothing can be done about unemployment. It was also helpful in establishing the 'credibility' of the Report, as can be seen from the coverage it received in the media. We recognise (p. 177) that the churches have no special expertise in economics, and we quote Archbishop Temple's view that *'Christian faith does not by itself enable its adherents to foresee how a vast multitude of people ... and an intricate economic mechanism will in fact be affected by a particular economic or political innovation.'* Nevertheless we reject the complete separation of questions of value and questions of fact (p. 82).

Christianity is obviously about values (about what ought to be) but it also presents a view of human nature (a view of what actually is) which contrasts quite sharply with that offered by economic theory. Conversely economists, although they are obviously concerned to find out how the world in fact works, do so within a framework of theory, which is itself also by implication normative. Christians cannot therefore simply 'subcontract' the working out of the economic implications of their faith to experts who do not share it. The economics and Christianity have to be brought together, ultimately by forming a common understanding of human nature and purpose. That is the direction in which the Report tries to point in various passages, but it remains a distant goal.

The main conclusions of the Report are briefly set out on page 2 of the summary. One way of stating our objective would be that full employment should be the aim, but that on its own, it is not enough. There must be good work for everyone to do. We assume that this aim is to be pursued within the context of an advanced market economy open to trade with the rest of the world. Given a high enough priority we believe that such an aim could be achieved, although it would take time and it would call for some sacrifice from those who are now prospering as a result of the same forces that have also created unemployment and low pay.

We favour changes in the structure of taxation to encourage employment in the private sector, most notably in services. We also favour increases in employment in such areas as health, education and construction. The long-term unemployed should be treated with generosity and be given help and encouragement so that they can take their rightful place in the mainstream of the economy. We deplore the development of a labour market in which pay and conditions of some are now 'insultingly' bad. We would counter this trend by supporting the introduction of a minimum wage and the strengthening of the bargaining position of the weak. Our

Report has been rightly interpreted as an appeal for the rich and secure to do more to help the poor and those excluded from society.

The Report was published during the UK General Election campaign. This may have offended some Christians, who have seen it as adopting an essentially partisan view. I hope we can convince them that this is a misunderstanding of the reasons behind the choice of publication date. It is certainly true that we directed our criticism at all the main political parties for neglecting the people who are in greatest need (p. 2). It is also undoubtedly the case that publishing when we did secured us a wider and more receptive audience than we could have secured at another time. Having made that initial impact, we are following up with a series of conferences and other meetings to present our Report in more detail to the churches and to society as a whole. This should be just the beginning of a long campaign.

I hope that *Unemployment and the Future of Work* may provide some valuable experience to the churches about how they can influence public opinion and policy. The fact that all of the main Christian denominations were in this together was itself no mean achievement, and a powerful demonstration of unity. Despite the difficulties, which I stressed at the beginning of this paper, we did show that some distinctively Christian beliefs and attitudes can be communicated effectively and be accepted by most people as a valuable contribution to public debate. In the process we may have helped to strengthen the self-confidence of the churches. I believe that we have also been preaching the gospel.

A Defence of *Unemployment and the Future of Work*

Ian Markham

Towards the end of the Report, we find the following: '*The ideas which we develop in this report are radical and they should be the subject of continuing debate and controversy.*'[1]. Radicalism is very definitely in the eye of the beholder. There are, at least, two types of radicalism. One type accepts a certain framework but takes a fairly extreme position within the framework; the other wants to challenge the entire framework and create new and different options outside the particular orthodoxy. We will call the first a 'tame radicalism' and the second 'outside radicalism'. For example, if you mix with a group of biblical fundamentalists, radicalism can mean doubting a literal six-day creation; this is a 'tame radicalism'. If, however, you interpret Genesis as myth and believe that a critical interpretation of the Bible needs to be accommodated by Christians, then you are, in respect to this particular issue, an outside radical.

In this Report you will find a 'tame radicalism'; it makes relatively minor suggestions within the framework of the dominant orthodoxy. The orthodoxy of today's politics is one that accepts the importance of the regulated market (p. 24). Left and right in British politics do not disagree about the necessity of regulation, only about its extent. The left would like to see more regulation and some Government intervention in the market, while the right wants to see less. However, this is not a disagreement of principle, but simply one of practice. It is worth recalling that this agreement is a remarkable phenomenon. Some like to give the credit to Thatcherism, but I am inclined to believe that the collapse of communism in the East has probably been a more decisive factor. The political and economic consensus in relation to the market is a given which the Report accepts.

Given the Report's endorsement of this economic orthodoxy, we find that the 'radicalism' consists of a call for greater regulation and some intervention. So, the Report recommends a minimum wage (p. 105), higher taxation (p. 96), and a unified system of benefits (p. 142). It was not surprising that both Will Hutton and Paddy Ashdown were very enthusiastic about the Report; it shared their radicalism, namely, that Government can and should do more to ameliorate the damaging impact of the market. However it is a radicalism which accepts the parameters of the market.

If you compare this 'tame radicalism' with the radicalism of those interested in Christian ethics within British Universities, you will find that the Report looks very tame indeed. Some of the most able scholars in Christian ethics today would want to reject the framework of the Report. Some would want to challenge the theological framework, while others would want to challenge the political framework. However, I shall show that the Report is right. Its 'tame radicalism' is in touch with the contemporary political agenda. In so doing, it ensures that it has an impact, and I suspect it will prove influential.

I shall now outline three contrasting approaches, available in current Christian ethical thinking. Two of them disagree strongly with the theology of the Report; the other would disagree with the politics. In each case, I shall outline the approach and attempt to imagine how it might produce a different report. I shall then defend the Report against these approaches. The three approaches are 1) the post-modern Augustinianism of John Milbank 2) the Barthian approach of Oliver O'Donovan and Michael Banner, and 3) the Green critique of conventional economics.[2]

The first approach is that of John Milbank. Everyone agrees that *Theology and Social Theory* is a remarkable book. The scale of his enterprise is breath-taking; and it is both informed and erudite. Milbank entirely rejects the Report's insistence that '*the churches have no special expertise to offer in the solution of economic problems*'.[3] For Milbank, this statement is poor philosophy as well as poor theology. The secular study of economics is based on a secular narrative, which is fundamentally at odds with the Christian narrative. When the Report distinguishes Christian expertise from the discipline of economics, it is ignoring the assumptions underpinning the study of economics. These assumptions are a result of a secular narrative that is opposed to the Christian meta-narrative. Milbank would presumably argue that the Report is philosophically confused because it fails to take historicism seriously and thereby grants an autonomy to the economic realm (and thus the market) that is not warranted. The Report becomes theologically confused because it denies the all-embracing nature of the Christian meta-narrative.

For Milbank, a Christian ecclesial contribution to the debate about unemployment would have been much more radical. Methodologically, he would have made theology much more central. Politically, his policies would have much more sympathy with the Green movement (see below). Milbank's 'Augustinian post-modernism' is in fact similar to the second approach, that of the Barthian realists.

Of the three Chairs of Christian Ethics in England (Oxford, London and Manchester), the first two are held by Barthian realists. In their writings Professors O'Donovan and Banner both argue for a much more overtly Christian ethic. Following Barth, they believe that ethics must be grounded in the Christian gospel. They would see nothing distinctively Christian about this report: its theology tends to come in platitudes - the vision of the kingdom, the image of God, work as contribution to community, and the dangers of turning the market into a God (p. 3-4). For O'Donovan and Banner, a Christian ethics must be grounded more overtly in the language of Christian dogmatics. So perhaps (and here I am only guessing what they might want to argue) a Christian understanding of work should draw upon the images of work applied to the different persons of Trinity. The Creator God works for six days and rests on the seventh; the Son works in redeeming human wickedness on the cross; and the Spirit works to illuminate the Church. No doubt from all this one could formulate a Trinitarian account of work that stresses initiative (God the Father), justice (God the Son) and ongoing creativity (God the Spirit).

Milbank's historicism arrives at the same place as O'Donovan's theology: both would dislike the Report because it is insufficiently Christian. The problem one has with both approaches is; how do you move from the philosophical-cum-theological mode of discourse to policy prescriptions? In *Plurality and Christian Ethics*, I argued that Christian ethics need to operate in three modes: the theological, the cultural, and the applied. A Christian ethic which cannot both shape a vision and suggest the means of attaining it is not much use. It seems to me that both Milbank and O'Donovan have no interest in constructing a meaningful practical social ethic for today. All they offer is an idealised vision of the Church that they insist should live out the truth of the Christian meta-narrative. This is the old dualism, where the Church is separated from the world and potentially has embedded in it a pietist gospel of social indifference.

The third approach, which the Report ignores, is the Green critique of the market. Ever since Mishan's book *The Costs of Economic Growth*,[4] there has been a growing movement opposed to the political orthodoxy that economic growth is part of the solution to most of our problems. The argument runs as follows: economic growth necessarily involves a range of effects, which ultimately the world cannot afford. This is not simply a reference to the depleting of the world's resources and pollution, but also the impact of large cities and mobility on the quality of human life. Plenty of Christians feel that there is considerable truth in this critique. A Report written from this perspective would stress the need for a radical overhaul of our political orthodoxy. We need to encourage smaller communities; the dependence of the motor car needs to be reduced; and work should be worthwhile and creative.

Much to my surprise this approach is largely ignored. Economic growth is indirectly commended. *'The economy needs to expand in directions which will create more and better jobs.'*[5] The Report mentions protectionism, as an option they were encouraged to endorse, but they reject it (p. 22). Although the quality of work is an issue, ecological questions are hardly ever raised.

Although it is a pity that the ecological dimension was not given more attention, there is much to be said for the view that economic growth is a wholly appropriate element in any proposed solution to unemployment. Naturally we have to be constantly vigilant about potential abuse of the environment. However, it may be that most of the problems generated by economic growth are, at the very least, ameliorated and sometimes solved by economic growth. However, there are elements of the Green analysis which are hostile to a Christian analysis. For example, calls for a decrease in the human population so that we can create more space for the rest of the creation to flourish are fine; suggestions from Garrett Hardin that this will involve not helping the developing nations of the world overcome their poverty are wicked.

So to sum up, in my view this is a good Report. It is a Report in conversation with policy makers. The Working Party has taken evidence from all of the major players and specialists. It is informed. I have no doubt that the Report's opponents would not have produced such a successful piece of work. It has made an impact, it will continue to have an impact, and I suspect a significant number of its recommendations will, over the course of the next five years, be implemented.

REFERENCES

1   *Unemployment and the Future of Work: An Enquiry for the Churches*, CCBI, 1997, p. 179.

2   The Green approach is not an exclusively Christian approach. However, there are many currently teaching Christian Ethics who are very sympathetic to Green arguments. See, for example, the journal *Theology in Green.*

3   *Unemployment and the Future of Work*, p.177.

4   Mishan. E.J. *The Costs of Economic Growth*, Staples Press, 1967.

5   *Unemployment and the Future of Work: An Enquiry for the Churches*, CCBI, 1997, p. 8.

How Can We Do Theology in Public Today?

Malcolm Brown

I want to begin this paper with two scenarios from the life of the Interim Sponsoring Group - the body that worked from 1993 to 1995 to establish the terms of reference and structure of the Unemployment and Future of Work project. One is verifiable by others, though sadly never minuted officially, the other purely my own impression borne out in informal conversations. Both, I believe, illustrate profound obstacles to doing theology on public issues today.

The first concerns a moment at the Bishop of Liverpool's house where we were trying to establish the membership of the Working Group. At one point in the debate we found ourselves seeking a working group that must include: women, men, black, white, employers, employed, unemployed, youth, business, trade union and financial interests, people from England, Scotland, Wales and Ireland, be denominationally representative, and no more than ten people. Clearly the process began with the observation that the Working Group should not be composed entirely of 'men in suits' - but the ever-growing list demonstrated the very serious sense in which the fragmentation of interest-groups, and the sharp awareness of the importance of diverse perspectives in 'doing theology', creates a context in which no-one may speak on behalf of a wider interest than their own. And like many nurtured in the liberal traditions - socially and theologically - we found that the tools for handling that plurality were not available. In a discussion of plurality as '*blessing and curse*' Max Stackhouse comments that '*[the] contributions by previously excluded peoples diversify and enrich ranges of life that may have spoken of pluralism but exemplified monolithic domination.*' But he goes on to say that the view that '*everything depends on ... the perspective from which we see it*' may lead to a dynamic pluralism, but one that '*cannot guide our thought or our lives in the cosmopolitan world of modern political economy*'.[1]

The second, more impressionistic, scenario amounts to the 'strange case of the dog that didn't bark'. Despite the presence around the table of representatives of most of the mainstream churches, there was no debate about different models of theological engagement, nor of the questions for public theology raised by our differing histories and practices of church/state relationships. One might have supposed that '*we are all liberal Anglicans now*'. But I suspect that the illusion of our commonality obscured the true plurality of the group and that resistance to a thoroughly plural social analysis runs very deep. And so the variety of possible theological approaches was ignored, leading perhaps to the 'confused' theological voice noted by Nigel Biggar[2]. (In fact a rather good example of diverse rationalities in theological reflection occurs in the Roman Catholic Bishops' Report, *The Common Good*,[3] where abortion is cited as a cause of the devaluation of human life and hence of social fragmentation - an argument which many Christians and others would want to put the other way around. And it seems very difficult to conceive of any model for bringing those two positions into any dialogue together under a common rationality.)

As a member of the Interim Sponsoring Group, my fear was that we had learned nothing from the reception given to *Faith in the City*[4] more than a decade ago: that to give a coherent sociological or economic apologia for the work was insufficient without a thoroughgoing theological case for the churches making an engagement with social and economic realities, and that a failure to be up front about the strengths and weaknesses of the chosen theological method could lead to the Report being disowned from within the churches, thereby legitimating a full-frontal attack from politicians and hostile media elements. Far from all being liberal Anglicans, now that the securities of establishment within a consensus are crumbling, it is more true to say that we are all dissenters these days. My 'Annexe I' at the end of the Report was written in order to try to put these concerns on the Working Group's agenda, rather than to act in any way as a final word to the Report.[5]

In the end, I think my fears were exaggerated but still reasonably well founded. The political atmosphere of the election campaign was very different to the strident Thatcher years into which *Faith in the City* was launched. And, in the end, as Nigel Biggar says, the Report's 'unmethodical method' is certainly not fatal. The Report says important things and says them well. What it does not do is help us much with the questions about the underpinning rationale for a public theology on economic and social issues - one which, as Stackhouse puts it, might be a *'capacious theology, defensible in public discourse, that is able to link personal and social matters, ideal and material reality, memory and hope, private and public vision.'*[6]

The problems of plurality for theological method

If we are justified in placing the Report within the Anglican Board of Social Responsibility tradition (despite its ecumenical imprint), then the challenge to that tradition needs to be spelt out. Although Henry Clark has called the Anglican Board of Social Responsibility *'one of the two most effective ecclesiastical social action groups operating in the world today'*[7] it is also a tradition challenged from the 'confessional' liberationist theologies of, for instance, Ulrich Duchrow,[8] for being too willing to treat with the powerful in a fatal compromise, and from the Christian communitarian positions (which, politically, may be of left or right) for whom it holds an inadequate theology of the uniqueness of the church. Both critiques call for a sharper sense of Christian distinctiveness and they might accept Digby Anderson's charge that the Board of Social Responsibility model reflects no more than the prejudices of the liberal intelligentsia (without necessarily accepting that Anderson offers a serious theological alternative).[9]

I want to argue that the shifting social context - and hence the priority of new questions for the churches - means that the issue of Christian distinctiveness needs to be addressed as part of a 'new settlement' for faith communities within a deeply plural, but not totally fragmented or relativistic, society. In other words, I believe that theologians like Michael Banner and John Milbank[10] are raising questions which demand answers and that their analysis of the plural social condition is acute. But I remain convinced that there are tools for addressing our condition which do not require either the dominance of a Christian grand narrative, the assertion of the Church's supremacy as a community of tradition, or the confinement of theological discourse to those of the household of faith, but which, rather, engage pilgrim Christian communities in dialogue with wider and diverse social ethics and perspectives on experience. As Raymond Plant says in a recent paper: *'Christians can share with non-Christians a concern with the importance of social justice and create a common agenda for a just social order. This will include specific values drawn from the churches' own ethical understanding but does not preclude collaboration with others.'*[11] Thus the ambitions of the Churches' Enquiry are endorsed, although questions of method remain.

The tradition of Social Christianity embodied by Temple emerged in a period of considerable social consensus. It's no accident that *Christianity and Social Order*[12] published in 1942 captured the public imagination as it did, nor that *Unemployment and the Future of Work* (p51) describes the social coherence forged in war time as the key to the next *twenty* years of full employment. In a relatively stable, consensual, society in which the Church (at least the Church of England) stood as one of the estates of the realm, the place of the Church 'at the table' did not need to be argued for, as it must be today (though, of course it only ever claimed one seat, not the chair of the meeting, as Milbank's attempt to rehabilitate a Christian Grand Narrative would presumably demand). The idea that around the table the theologian might be essentially unintelligible to the economist was not seen as a serious possibility. But, as my first scenario seems to suggest, the plurality of perspectives, and the absence of a single unifying narrative, makes dialogue particularly difficult. The Report itself brushes against this problem when it says that we must listen particularly to the voices of unemployed people. Implicit in this statement are assumptions about who 'we' are, and are not, and about the privileging of certain perspectives above others. If these assumptions were explored further, they would not only lead directly into the problems of diversity and perspective, but would also lead to real difficulties about the composition and methods of the Working Group, the ownership of the Report itself, and the ability of this model of theological engagement to handle a plural context.

However, I want to go further and echo Alasdair MacIntyre's dystopian vision in the first chapter of *After Virtue*[13], in which he describes the incommensurability of moral positions in a world which has come to the end of the Enlightenment project. Unless we take a similarly robust view of the plural nature of society we will continue to regard diversity as an aberration and, in asserting ever more stridently our liberal positions, succeed only in demonstrating the illiberalism of which illiberal people like Anderson accuse us.

Plurality and Communities

One problem in adopting MacIntyre's analysis of plurality is that his excursion into an ethic of tradition, practice and virtue leaves us hanging on the final paragraph of *After Virtue* pondering the call for new forms of community generated, perhaps, by a new St Benedict. Nothing in MacIntyre's subsequent writings, with their deeper commitment to a Thomist ethic, really tells us how such new communities might co-exist - at least if they are to be at all diverse. And although he rejects the appellation for himself, MacIntyre's work has given much impetus to communitarianism. While the arch-apostle of communitarianism,

Etzioni,[14] is wonderfully ambiguous about the scale of community (is it the neighbourhood? the interest group? the nation? - in other words, the 'who is 'we'' question) - Christian communitarians, like Hauerwas, are very clear about their focus on the Church as the place of values and virtues, and the Church as the arena in which moral issues are played out. Hauerwas says *'the first task of the Church is not to supply theories of government legitimacy or even to suggest strategies for social betterment. The first task of the Church is to exhibit in [its] common life the kind of community possible when trust, and not fear, rules our lives'*.[15] If that is true, then, in a plural world, communities are only able to speak coherently among themselves, and a project like *Unemployment and the Future of Work* becomes inconceivable.

I prefer to go back to MacIntyre who, I think, is saying something much less exclusive about new forms of community. When he speaks of shifting between one moral world and another as being like *'learning a second first language'*, and when he discusses *'Epistemological Crises'*,[16] he makes it clear that the boundaries between narratives, communities and interest groups are permeable. Hauerwas seems not to recognise this permeability and, as Plant points out, ignores the way that the Church's freedom to witness depends on the sort of democratic society that can only be secured through collaboration across community boundaries.[17]

The questions, therefore, are: how can communities and traditions be the location for moral and ethical practice (the distinctive identity question) and be open to dialogue across the boundaries of difference in ways which own, but do not absolutise, any particular moral discourse (the community-among-communities question)? As Ian Markham points out in his paper,[18] the neo-orthodox Barthian approach and the post-modern Augustinian 'Christendom' approach are strong on the first question but have no helpful way forward on the second. Peter Selby's recent book, *Grace and Mortgage*, arrives at a similar set of questions. Following Bonhoeffer's question *'Who is Jesus Christ for us today?'*, Selby develops three questions: *'who we are? (the question of identity), who 'us' is? (the question of solidarity) and whose 'today' is it to be? (the challenge of discernment)'*[19]. These are very helpful, although I think Selby's third question entails 'boundary negotiations' in a more central place than he recognises.

Plurality and Economics

It may be worth, at this point, adding a note about why this Report's subject-matter - or rather, the economy generally - is such an important case-study for an emerging new theological method. Plurality is a challenge as much to economics as to theology, and so a theological response ought to be testable according to the amount of light it sheds on the economist's struggle with plurality. In this sense, I think the Report does not really grapple enough with the moral philosophy that informs rival economic viewpoints.

Margaret Thatcher's economic experiment was not a political aberration but a genuine, if unbalanced, attempt to address the problem of the distribution of goods in a plural context. This was the moral problem to which the amoral market offered the only solution that was not immoral. Any more *dirigiste* approach to distribution was condemned as the imposition of the values and preferences of an elite. The way in which the Report handles the idea of taxation is instructive. It rightly emphasises that taxation levels are a matter of political prioritising, and it recognises that the political process requires consent - a consent that it locates in a revitalised understanding of a common good. But the point made by the free-marketeers is that where a perception of the common good is insufficiently widely held, taxation for redistributive ends is a form of coercion. And not only the free-marketeers, but also the pluralists and the MacIntyrians are clear that no such consensus on the common good is currently available to us.

Raymond Plant has spent a lot of time since *Faith in the City* challenging the churches to take this point seriously. In the face of the sustained demolition of the concept of the 'common good' from Robert Nozick through Freidrich Hayek to Keith Joseph[20] and beyond, it just is not sufficient to assert that such a thing as the 'common good' exists and can be agreed upon. This is part of the objection to the economic elements of Etzioni's communitarianism - that in the end he asserts distributional solutions on majoritarian grounds (and explicitly moral majoritarian grounds), and so fails to secure the diversity that guarantees economic freedom (on a limited, but important, view of freedom).

The coverage of the churches' *Unemployment* Report in *The Daily Telegraph*[21] over-reached itself by using this argument to label the Report 'communist' - but that does not render the argument itself negligible. I think that the hesitation expressed by Tony Blair about the Report when it was published - to the effect that the encouragement of higher taxation ignored the political realities - was an acknowledgement of the strength of the moral argument for markets and the perception that redistributive taxation does not enjoy an adequate mandate. And this is not just about a lack of political will or an uneducated or unreflective electorate. It is about deep structural divisions in society and in the grounds of people's ethical reasoning. The politics of plurality are severely limited in their ability to reflect or regenerate a concept of the 'common good'.

Nonetheless, irreducible market individualism is not the last word. Fred Hirsch, Plant[22] and others have demonstrated the extent to which the market itself relies upon elements of social solidarity, shared values and common ethics, and that, despite the pretensions of the free-marketeers, these factors are not 'given' but must either be engendered through consent or imposed through authoritarianism. Even if the latter course has tended to stain government practice over the last eighteen years, it remains that the generation of limited agreement about the ethics of distribution between diverse moral communities is conceivable and so may not be limited to the residual levels of agreement that lie behind free-market economics. In other words, if a degree of social cohesion is required by the market to function at all, and if that cohesion can be secured freely, then socially agreed goods (a limited version of a 'common good') are constrained only by the practical limits of social agreement - which may be severely constrained now, but are not necessarily so. The 'common good' cannot be asserted, but it can be approached in negotiated dialogue.

Seeking a Distinctive Process of Engagement

In this, an approach to theological method does shed some light, and I am indebted to Ian Markham's book *Plurality and Christian Ethics*[23] for getting me thinking on these lines. Along with Markham in his paper, I want to reject the positions which he attributes to Milbank, Banner and O'Donovan, and for the same reasons - that they are insufficiently dialogical in their approach to other traditions, practices and communities of virtue and thus insufficiently open to being changed - a factor which, in the limited revelation of 'the interim' between Pentecost and the Parousia, ought surely to be an indispensable element of any Christian position. Nevertheless, a plural social analysis means that we cannot afford to lose sight of the question of Christian distinctiveness although I do not understand distinctiveness in quite the way Banner or Milbank would. Again, who are 'we'? Markham is right that this is a Report 'in conversation with policy-makers' - but it is not quite about the Church in conversation with policy makers or theology in conversation with economics. And this is surely because the Report achieved its public credibility largely from the credentials of its Executive Secretary and main author as an economist of note. The fact that the economic literacy of the Report has brought it, relatively unscathed, into the public domain is to be welcomed, but by this process a Christian economist of another hue (perhaps a Brian Griffiths or even a Michael Novak) would have written a very different Report that could have been just as much the 'voice of the churches'. The Report contains some distinctively Christian reflections and some distinctive economics - but it doesn't link them in any way that allows us to find here a distinctively Christian approach to economics. What is needed is some way of doing publicly what Andrew Britton embodies personally. But of course this opens up the problems of diversity and plurality in a much deeper way. So although the processes of the Working Group have produced a fascinating Report which has been received respectfully, they haven't established any methodology that is of wider application in more stridently contested issues than (surprisingly perhaps) unemployment turned out to be. We still need a better theory of Christian social engagement. What might it look like?

A Way Forward?

Unless we know who 'we' are we bring nothing to the dialogue process. But unless we are open to revising our self-definition in the light of dialogue, we bring to the encounter only an immovable object (and this, I think, is a paradox of Milbank's rejection of the ontology of violence). 'We', whoever 'we' are, are always in some way a coalition and a compromise. The 'we' who is the Church (certainly the 'we' of CCBI) is patently so. If we seek distinctiveness in a belief or position that is shared by no-one else we will, I suspect, be very lonely. The components of a distinctively Christian position on unemployment, which Markham in his paper postulates as a Barthian response, are not (insofar as they might manifest themselves in practice) individually unique to Christians. Only the use of elements of the Christian tradition as the foundations of a position is distinctively Christian, and this is not really very helpful in shaping a practice of engagement. Instead, I would seek distinctively Christian elements more in process than in propositions. In particular, the commitment to dialogue, to being open to change as well as seeking to bring about change, and to alliances, coalitions and networks. Also, the commitment to theology as, in Andrew Shanks' words, *'the opposite of ideology'*, the opposite of Augustine's *libido dominandi*.[24] And I would ground these commitments, less in the character of God or of Jesus Christ than in the character of the times - the 'interim' during which sin persists alongside the reality of God among us, in which we know partially rather than directly and in which all our best efforts contain within them fatal flaws, which necessitate constant re-balancing, compromise and revision (something recognised, I think, in the Pastoral Cycle approach to *praxis*).

And if a re-focusing on identity questions can lead in this way into new, negotiated alliances, then we are relieved of a good deal of anxiety about moving too far towards specific policy preferences. This Report is very specific about policy - and that is, again, because of the particular relationship between Andrew Britton as economist and as Executive Secretary of the project. Unpack these questions of role and identity and we may have the essence of a dialogic alliance methodology.

Developing a public theology within plurality must, I suspect, be always about an experimental practice rather than a watertight theory. An approach based on process and practice allows one to talk about practical possibilities and the limits of a partial consensus and the search for a 'shared ethic for now'. Any wider claim is too easily falsifiable - because someone or other is always going to be outside the dialogue, destroying any claim of universalisation. Habermas' view of consensus produced from '*intersubjective communicative action*' rather than '*a unity of experience*' might be helpful here if his own claims of universalism were less bold.

So the result, in terms of an approach to public theology, would draw on MacIntyre's account of communities of tradition and virtue, in order to recognise what we can bring to an encounter; on Andrew Shanks' development of the idea of *isonomy*, to establish a framework for collaborative relationships based on maintaining the '*direct spontaneous participation of every kind of person in public affairs*'; and on what Jeffrey Stout calls '*moral bricolage*'[25] as a model for assembling a position that can generate a degree of consensus which recognises its contingency and the centrality of alliances. Such an approach would not treat 'the Christian tradition' as one thing but as something ambiguous and paradoxical about which Christians themselves do not wholly agree. The fascination is in exploring the extent to which those approaching an issue from other traditions, experiences and interests can make common cause with Christians. If the residents of Mobberly and Knutsford could work in a constructive and mutually supportive alliance with the diggers and tunnellers under Manchester's second runway, then surely few alliances are inconceivable - so long as no-one expects the alliance to take the same shape if the next issue should be the Wilmslow by-pass. Indeed, there is much to learn from Rainbow Coalitions and New Social Movements about the nature of temporary alliances geared to achieving limited goals, rather than the 'search for unity' or for 'definitive positions' which has tended to characterise the tradition of Christian social engagement until now.

This may mean letting go of some cherished images of the Church as society's moral guardian, but that is a necessary preliminary to a genuine engagement with a fragmented society. But whilst MacIntyre calls the present condition of moral debate *'civil war conducted by other means'*, Stout reminds us that civil war by other means is greatly preferable to civil war itself, in which one version of morality achieves dominance over another by violence and bloodshed.[26]   Seeking to 'out-narrate' rival, inferior narratives, will not do; nor will the assertion of a 'common good' that it is not very widely perceived to be 'good for me'. But a theological engagement with a public issue like unemployment must be clear how it understands its Christian identity and its methodology of engagement if it is to be heard in the world or in the Church. As Markham's paper points out, the dominant trends in the theological part of the academy are much more radical than the theology of the Report, and the voices from the academy must be heard, not for themselves, but because they are addressing the problems of a context for the analysis of which there are few adequate tools. The context is that of our plurality, and whilst the churches may trade on their capital from an older dispensation a little longer, they will not be able to do so indefinitely.

When this Enquiry was first conceived, I feared that if we didn't demonstrate that we had learned from the theological critiques of *Faith in the City* we would never again have the confidence - or the authority - to tackle social affairs in the public sphere. I shall now have to say that about the next such project - we got away with it this time. I celebrate the Report for doing that - and doing it with panache. But how will we answer when it is once again more expedient for politicians and commentators to stress our social plurality and lack of consensus than to fudge them?

I believe that Christian engagement with the social and economic can be done in public - that our theology is not just for our own consumption - but that to do so requires much more work to be done on our own identity so that our 'dialogue partners' in other disciplines, and with different perspectives on the world, know who they are in dialogue with and on what terms.

REFERENCES

1   Max Stackhouse, *Public Theology and Political Economy*,
    University Press of America, 1992, p.158.

2   Nigel Biggar, 'Where there's a Will' in *Third Way*, May 1997.

3   Catholic Bishops' Conference of England and Wales, *The Common
    Good*, 1996. See especially para. 67.

4   The Archbishop's Commission on Urban Priority Areas, *Faith in
    the City*, Church House Publishing, 1985.

5   Malcolm Brown, 'Unemployment and the Future of Work; Some
    Thoughts on Theological Method' in *Unemployment and the Future
    of Work: An Enquiry for the Churches*, CCBI, 1997.

6   Stackhouse, *Public Theology*, 1992, p.2.

7   Henry Clark, *The Church Under Thatcher*, SPCK, 1993, p.1.

8   See, for example, Ulrich Duchrow, *Global Economy: A
    Confessional Issue for the Churches?* WCC, 1987.

9   See particularly: Digby Anderson, *The Kindness that Kills*, SPCK,
    1984.

10 See for example: Michael Banner, 'Nothing to Declare' in *The
    Church Times*, 16 June 1995.

    John Milbank, *Theology and Social Theory*, Blackwell, 1990.

11 Raymond Plant, 'Civic Virtue, Poverty and Social Justice' in,
    (ed) Peter Askonas and Stephen F Frowen, *Welfare and Values:
    Challenging the Culture of Unconcern.* Macmillan, 1997. p.281f.

12 William Temple, *Christianity and Social Order*, Penguin, 1942.

13 Alasdair MacIntyre, *After Virtue: A Study in Moral Theory*,
    Duckworth, 2nd ed., 1985.

14   See: Amitai Etzioni, *The Spirit of Community*. Fontana (Harper Collins), 1993.

    See also: Gerard Kelly, 'Off-the-shelf sociology', in *The Times Higher Education Supplement*, 24 March, 1995.

    Joan Smith, 'Should we live this way?' in *The Independent on Sunday*. 22 June 1997

15   Stanley Hauerwas, *A Community of Character*, Notre Dame, 1981. Quoted by Plant in *Civic Virtue, Poverty and Social Justice*, p.219.

16   See: Alasdair MacIntyre 'Epistemological Crises, Dramatic Narrative, and the Philosophy of Science', in (ed) Stanley Hauerwas *Why Narrative?* Grand Rapids, 1989, pp.138-157.

17   See: Plant, *Civic Virtues, Poverty and Social Justice*. 1997.

18   Ian Markham, *A Defence of Unemployment and the Future of Work*, 1997.

19   Peter Selby, *Grace and Mortgage*, DLT, 1997. p.119.

20   See for example:
    Robert Nozick, *Anarchy, State and Utopia*, Blackwell, 1974
    F Hayek, *Law, Legislation and Liberty, Vol 2 'The Mirage of Social Justice'*, Routledge and Kegan Paul, 1976.
    Keith Joseph, *Equality*, John Murray 1977.

21   Paul Goodman 'Socialism at Last' in *The Daily Telegraph*, 9 May 1997.

22   See: Fred Hirsch, *Social Limits to Growth*, Routledge and Kegan Paul, 1977.

    Raymond Plant, 'Conservative Capitalism; Theological and Moral Challenges' in (ed.) Anthony Harvey, *Theology in the City*, SPCK 1989.

23   Ian Markham, *Plurality and Christian Ethics*, CUP, 1994.

24   Andrew Shanks, '*A Theological Context for Urban/Industrial
      Mission*', privately circulated paper, 1996.
      See also: Andrew Shanks, *Civil Society, Civil Religion*, Blackwell,
      1995.

25   Jeffrey Stout, *Ethics After Babel*, Beacon Press, Boston, 1988.
      Stout defines 'Moral bricolage' as: "The process in which one
      begins with bits and pieces of received linguistic material, arranges
      some of them into a structured whole, leaves others to the side, and
      ends up with a moral language one proposes to use", ibid. p.294.

26   Stout, *Ethics After Bábel*, p.224.

A Comment on Method

Ronald Preston

This Report, published in April 1997, was the first effort of its kind by the Council of Churches for Britain and Ireland. It has been generally well received by its constituency and by a wider public, and deservedly so. Presumably its aim was twofold: (1) to arouse the Christian conscience, dulled by the relative prosperity of the majority, to the scandal of youth and long term unemployment experienced by a minority; (2) to influence a wider public and especially policy makers, and to indicate ways of tackling the problem. With respect to the first objective it is successful in bringing home the urgency of the problem, not least by meeting the unemployed and letting them tell their own story. As to the second objective, whilst I applaud the Report, there are some underlying questions about its method which need to be considered.

It is concerned with Church guidance, not that of a Freelance Think Tank. It has a certain, not precisely defined, Church status. In dealing with contemporary issues in any area churches have to bring their biblical and theological resources alongside empirical data. They are not entirely on their home ground; the data cannot be obtained from their internal resources. The data of whatever problem is under discussion has to be obtained by investigation and evaluated. In this process there are inevitable uncertainties of fact and interpretation. Opinions will differ. How can this best be handled?

I have thought for a long time that the best method has three stages. (1) Identify the problem. This involves a negative judgement on the *status quo*. Christians have a radical faith. They are taught not to be satisfied with things as they are and in particular to be sensitive to all who are marginalised, so they are not likely to lack issues to take up. (2) Get at the 'facts' by searching for the relevant evidence from those involved in the problem, whether as expert witnesses or as experiencing it personally. (3) Try to arrive at a broad consensus on what should be done - first of all at a middle level. This indicates a general direction at which policy should aim. Since there are always disagreements on public policies, among Christians, no less than the general public, this puts the onus on the objector if a Church Report can produce agreement on a general direction on policy. If it chooses, a Church Report can go on to recommend detailed policies, though the more detailed they are the more likely they are to be affected by the inevitable uncertainties in obtaining facts; these can often be evaluated and interpreted differently. Still more are the uncertainties in forecasting the effects of any detailed policies that are advocated. (Before asking how this recent Churches' Report looks in the light of this method, it is worth pointing out that if the empirical investigation proves so contentious that no broad agreement can be reached, the most constructive thing for a Commission to do is to define the different stances that Christians are taking to the evidence and then ask adherents of each to formulate the questions they want to put to the adherents of the others, and thus continue the dialogue between Christians).

The Report has successfully carried out stages one and two. It has passed a negative judgement on our present economic relative prosperity and vindicated its judgement that the level of unemployment is a scandal. As to stage three, it has arrived at a middle level judgement (though it does not call it that) that jobs must be found, and not any jobs, but good jobs. It puts forward a strong case. But it fails to put forward a point of view that continually finds expression among Christians (and, of course, others) who are alert to the evil of unemployment. They argue, either that technological development makes full employment impossible, so that the remedy involves, for instance, starting work later in life, retiring earlier and job sharing, or that the broadly free market is incapable of providing full employment, (it can be called Satanic) and needs to be replaced by a new economic order (very vaguely outlined).

There is, and has been for decades, a steady stream of books by individual Christians, Christian groups and people from other faiths and philosophies on these lines. How can this be dealt with? It involves an attitude to economics as an academic discipline. Its foundation is a study of the basic problems any society has to solve because of the human situation where we have relatively scarce resources compared with all the different things we might wish to do with them; choices have to be made. (In the last resort there are absolute scarcities, but that is not the immediate issue). Economists differ; like scholarship in any other academic discipline, there are schools of thought. But there is no difference among them that, in principle, full employment is possible - allowing for temporary unemployment in a dynamic and changing society. The Report is quite right. But it should have taken on the arguments of this persistent Christian undercurrent, which refuses to take economics seriously. It is indeed tedious to have to go on doing this decade after decade, but it needs doing. The Report has a very strong case for its claim that good jobs must be created to tackle the evil of unemployment. Theology cannot make the case by itself. Theologians have to leave their biblical and theological homeground and cope with the relative autonomy of economics.

When it comes to its more detailed proposals the Report does not face a broad division of opinion among those who think that full employment is possible and desirable. Some think the broadly free market system - the only one on offer since the internal collapse of the Soviet style command economies - can do this best if it is left to get on with least government interference; and there are those who think, on the other hand, that it cannot work satisfactorily without it being set within a strong framework of social policies which help citizens to cope with the stresses of dynamic change. The Report clearly takes the latter view; rightly, in my opinion. But it does not face the issue clearly. To do so, of course, would bring it into the heart of current politics, but it would have helped Christians to think out more fully the implications of political choices they are bound to make if unemployment is to be dealt with.

The theological comments on the Report that I have heard have not dealt with the points I have been making. It is understandable that theologians should work within the biblical and theological traditions in which they are at home, but they do also need to acknowledge the necessity of working with others and the problems this creates.

The theological comments I have heard have been on two lines. (1) Examining whether the theology of the Report is adequate, or whether the model, or various models, of the Church implied in it are adequate; and whether it deals adequately with some current tendencies in social theology. Such questions have their importance. Clearly some theologies are more adequate than others, and some are deplorable; but they are secondary to the primary question: 'Has the Report produced a cogent case at the middle and also at the detailed level?' (2) A concern whether the Report is sufficiently distinctively Christian. This again is a secondary question to the basic one about the Report. Obviously the Christian basis of its work needs to be made clear, but where the cogency of its recommendations is concerned - how peculiarly Christian they are, is a secondary question. Indeed, in a search for allies to influence public policy, it is to be hoped that others will agree with it. There is a tendency among some Christians to exaggerate the difficulties of getting agreement on policy in a plural society. Pluralism is not the same as fissiparousness.

I think the Report has produced a cogent argument at the third stage, which deserves an informed Church imprimatur from the churches that commissioned it. The General Synod of the Church of England in effect did this in July 1997. This puts the onus on objectors to the Report rather than its advocates. I hope it shifts Christian opinion and also public opinion. But it would have been better if its method had been clearer.

The Ecclesiology of *Unemployment and the Future of Work*

Elaine Graham

I am sure the authors of this Report are a little tired of its being compared with the Church of England report on the inner cities, *Faith in the City*, which caused so much controversy during the 1980s.[1] But I think that *Faith in the City* has come to be seen as the defining moment in contemporary theological thinking on social and economic affairs and in Church/State relations, and as a benchmark against which, inevitably, all successive documents are to be judged. That is not to lionise excessively the insights or the legacy of *Faith in the City*: it did have its flaws.[2] But I think it was significant for two main reasons, both of which, in a way, I hope this Report is able to emulate.

Firstly, it did have a significant impact on public thinking and policy around its chosen theme. So if *Unemployment and the Future of Work* can create and generate the same level and quality of public debate as *Faith in the City* did, then all well and good.

But the second significant feature of *Faith in the City* was that it provided food for thought of a more academic nature - 'academic' not, as sometimes occurs, as a term of abuse ('irrelevant', 'unreasonably esoteric and inaccessible'), but in terms of stimulating Christians to be critical and reflective, as well as encouraging them to be practical and effective. In particular, I think *Faith in the City* enabled theologians and the churches to think more deeply about the nature of theological understanding of contemporary society; what theological sources and norms might be deployed in the pursuit of social action; the importance of what Ronald Preston has called *'Christian competence'*[3]: informed, judicious empirical work which really gets to grips with the facts of the matter. *Unemployment and the Future of Work* stands honourably in that tradition in its rigorous and expert treatment of the economic and fiscal dimensions of taxation, welfare, investment and job creation.

As Malcolm's paper, and other contributions have noted, however, there is less clarity and rigour when it comes to the problems of articulating a public theology in a context of economic and religious pluralism. As Malcolm said in his paper about the Report: *'... there was no debate about different models of theological engagement, nor of the questions for public theology raised by the different histories and practices of church/state relationships.'* I find it significant that Malcolm has chosen to link together here the question of the nature of theological discourse (who does it, where it comes from and whether it can have critical and creative bearing on other world-views and discourses) and the nature and self-understanding of the Church and the world.

So whilst Malcolm's paper concentrates on identifying and analysing several alternative theological models via the positions of particular protagonists, I want to take another look at this issue by asking what models of the Church inform this Report: what is the ecclesiology of the Report, its understanding of 'Church' both as sociological and theological realities?

In focusing on the ecclesiology of the Report, I do not want to reduce all theological thinking to that generated by the Church, or to endorse a pre-modern, post-Milbankian notion of some self-sufficient Christian narrative. But I do want to argue that we cannot separate the generation of theological discourse from its sociological and institutional locations - be that Church, society or academy. All theology, like any other kind of knowledge, comes from somewhere; and knowing something of the context of the claims of theology enables us to reach a more judicious assessment of it.

In this respect, *Unemployment and the Future of Work* can also learn from *Faith in the City,* in the sense that the theological statements and tenor of the latter were crucially dependent on the nature of the Church from which they emanated. I think the theology of *Faith in the City,* for all its flaws, actually emerged from a very particular ecclesiological and sociological understanding of what it means to be 'Church': in this case, of course, Church of England. It was, I believe, the peculiar parochial and constitutional position of the Church of England that was largely responsible for the character and impact of *Faith in the City.* The genius of *Faith in the City* was that a middle-class, rural/suburban church, thoroughly implicated in the establishment, should still produce a statement on urban priority areas that challenged prevailing policy and emerged as the advocate and champion of the poor. But that is not really a result of the insights of liberation theology, despite the much-debated and vaunted Theological Chapter in that document. Actually, it is due to a much more profoundly 'contextual' theology: the parish system and a good old Anglican tradition of incarnational theology of presence, embodied in day-to-day ministry, is what ultimately lends *Faith in the City* its gloriously subversive authority.[4]

But the Archbishop's Commission on Urban Priority Areas was able to speak with subversive authority because it based its findings on experiences from a particular ecclesial and political position, which actually shaped its convictions and informed its public statements. The presence of Church of England congregations, plant and professionals in inner-city areas come what may, constituted a kind of compact between Church and people which illustrated and exemplified the historic mission of the Church of England to be the Church for and of the nation far more graphically than any theological statements ever could.

One element of the debate, which we have already been charting, is the argument as to whether theological discourse can still (if ever it did) presume to attain an authoritative, binding or even primary role in public policy. However, one of the lessons we are learning as a result of a realisation of pluralism in lifestyle, values and epistemology, is that all knowledge comes from somewhere. At one level, this is exemplified by the protests of postmodernism that no account of human experience or destiny is neutral or privileged; there is no 'grand narrative' under which the diversities and particularities of life can be subsumed. We all tell our own stories; we must now see knowledge and perspectives as local, situated and contingent. As Malcolm's discussion notes, this seeming collapse of moral unanimity, so influentially articulated by Alasdair MacIntyre, gives rise to dilemmas about the future possibility of social and moral consensus and community. On what principles can shared ideals of justice and progress rest 'after Babel'? Some philosophers and theologians, following MacIntyre, turn to communitarian models; we are united by the stories we tell, and our common life results from the discharge of such narratives. A number of theologians are resolving the challenges of cultural and religious pluralism by propounding a model of theology as essentially the public utterance of Christian self-understanding, constituting coherent and binding truth-claims as practised by particular communities of faith in a concrete context, time and place.

Theology can, I believe, be a vital resource in the renewal of society's shared vocabulary. But theology has human agents, who cannot pretend to be voices from nowhere; they actually have more credibility if they point to the experiences, challenges and struggles out of which those theological principles and truth-claims have arisen. And that means the day-to-day activities of communities of faith: worship, pastoral care, social action. In other words, theology begins and ends in Christian practice or, if you prefer, *praxis*, as denoting value-laden and value-directed activity. This perspective is associated with contemporary movements of contextual theology, such as Liberation Theology, but it is also true to earlier traditions and remains an important strand of theological thinking. If theological values have any substance, they will exist in primary form as faithful practices - pastoral care, worship, social action - and only derivatively as doctrines and concepts. So it is thus in the dynamics and practices of faithful community that Christians embody their truth-claims.

So if we actually look to see what models of 'being Church' and of *'praxis'* are actually present in this Report, I think we would find an amazing kaleidoscope of practical engagement from which some important criteria for effective and faithful Christian intervention and involvement might be derived. But we have to understand, I think, that such evidence conceals a wide variety of implicit assumptions about why Christians should be involved in society, to what ends.

Firstly, although the prospect of individual witness and ministry is mentioned (p. 175), it is hardly developed; we have little idea of what the Christian is witnessing to. So personal evangelism does not feature in this model of Church in the world. More firmly rejected is the idea of Church as 'sanctuary or haven' from social and moral issues. *'In times of rapid social change and insecurity, churches and other religious institutions are often seen as places of refuge in which people can shelter and find comfort'* (p. 30). But the Church has a responsibility to embrace the future and foster the Kingdom. *'It is all too easy for the Church to retreat into a private sphere, to become an escape route from the world and not a means of redeeming it'* (p. 10).

So here we seem to have a fundamental understanding of the Church which is the vehicle and source of Christian activity as institutional presence at many points of the worlds of work, industry, unemployment and politics. But clearly, the Church of this Report is not content with words; actions feature prominently, for example, in the section, *'Mobilising Our Resources'* (pp. 180-194). So, for starters, the Church is seen as 'service provider': practical provision, such as Employment Projects, counselling or rights and advice work. The churches here engage with the wider community primarily as voluntary organisations: *'The churches are providing action as well as words'* (p.10). *'Community Employment Projects'* (p. 193); opportunities for volunteering, job clubs, job creation, project work, campaigning and lobbying bodies such as

43

Church Action on Poverty (CAP) or the Churches Unemployment Group (CHUG). We are also reminded that, historically speaking, the churches have always been providers of training and education (p. 145).

Another model is that of 'presence': the Church in the local neighbourhood, or represented in the workplace via kinds of sector ministry such as Industrial Mission (IM). However, there is ambivalence over IM (pp. 186-189) as there is within the wider Church which further suggests that the ecclesiology of the Report - the relationship between 'Church' as committed congregation, sector chaplains, Diaspora of lay ministers and so on - is underdeveloped.

Another model is that of 'advocate', on behalf of the unemployed or poor. But the impression given is that 'Church' and 'unemployed' are separate constituencies: not the intention of the Report, I know, but a trap into which it falls nonetheless: *'Church leaders have been able on occasion to speak in national policy debates on behalf of the powerless ... people living in poverty ... had the opportunity to describe their way of life to an audience of leaders in Church and community.'* (p. 178). I am not castigating the churches for being 'middle-class'; but merely pointing out that this model of how Church membership, leadership and community interact reflects a very particular, but not universal situation. A similar emphasis emerges from the model of Church as 'community of expertise', containing many people with power and influence in society. *'The churches also have influence because they include in their membership many in positions of power and responsibility in government, business, trade unions and other organisations.'* (p. 178). However, if these two models are to be taken together, they present one particular model of who and what (sociologically and theologically) the Church is: drawn from the privileged and powerful, seeking to address those in government and authority who are similar to themselves. The discussion of the 'Wood-Sheppard principles' on good practice around promoting racial equality in employment (p. 116) thus portrays the churches as honest brokers, a 'sponsor' of policy, underwriting and implementing equal opportunities.

This model of the Church at work may well be politically realistic; but I think it shows how far the Report lapses into Anglican thought-forms, which inevitably shapes its assumptions about how the churches can intervene in, and influence, political decision-making. It reflects an ecclesiology of a Church which is aware of its marginal place in the hearts and minds of many, but is confident still of its seat at the table of power. But are there not alternative ecclesiologies, of dissent and non-conformity, of solidarity with the powerless? Where do we hear traditions of Church as suffering servant, of struggle against powerlessness and oppression, of the importance of 'holiness' amidst hardship, characteristic of some Black-majority traditions?

The Church is also conceived of as *Guardian* or *Repository*: of values, insights and perspectives from *'the Christian tradition'*: *'There is an abundance of wisdom in scripture, in the teaching of the early fathers of the Church and the writings of numerous Christian thinkers down the ages'* (p. 5). However, diversity and disagreement in tradition is not considered; rather, theological traditions appear homogeneous and uniform. The strands of teaching alluded to in *Unemployment and the Future of Work* - the common good (p. 51), inclusive community (p. 53) and the work ethic (p. 71) - owe a great deal to their Christian origins, but these are assumed to be normative and definitive. This is therefore a tradition which is self-evident and unproblematic: *'debate amongst Christians about the meaning of the Gospel and also debate with others in society about the application of the values we hold in common.'* (p. 10): so there is unanimity not just about the Christian tradition, but how it is to be preserved, handed down and communicated. This is where the notion of theology as articulating commonly held principles is clearest: *'Our own aim is not partisan. It is to help set the agenda, to prick the national conscience, by raising the saliency of unemployment as an issue, and to ask the public as a whole to accept the responsibility for effective practical remedies which will be costly to themselves.'* (p. 10).

The Church is also portrayed as a teller of stories: linked with guardian of tradition and insights, but it is interesting to note how Biblical and historical narrative is inserted to illustrate a point, e.g. the story of Israelites captive in Egypt forced to make bricks without straw as an illustration of unfair employment practices! So not only is the Church a source of particular values, but a resource for the telling of stories from a particular body of wisdom (p. 150).

The model of Church as worshipping congregation is also given a fair degree of attention. This is particularly relevant in relation to references to Unemployment Sunday, but emerging, significantly, towards the very end of the Report in some very different reflections on the importance - or even primacy - of worship (p. 194). There are two particularly interesting strands to this: firstly, we see a model of Church as local congregation focused on the ministry of the Word: *'Church mission to the world of work must be founded on belief and action at this local level, on prayer, on praise and on fellowship in Christ'* (p. 190). Secondly, we have a much more Eucharistic and sacramental understanding of Church - again, arguing that it is at its gathering for worship that the Church most authentically enacts its truth-claims: *'Our main concern is that the world of work should be taken right into the heart of Christian life, which is the main Sunday service that most Church members attend ... In many churches the main service on Sunday morning is a celebration of the Eucharist or Holy Communion ... The offering of bread and wine to be transformed into the body and blood of Christ is a symbol of the offering of all our lives'* (p. 194).

Now, those two models of Church reflect very different emphases. In practice, they would be representative not of one uniform tradition, but hold in tension a wide spectrum of theological and ecclesiological understandings: but I don't think that the diversity and heterogeneity of Christian experience is fully acknowledged or valued.

I think the Report does mine a rich seam of Church-related *praxis*, and does implicitly acknowledge that a theology of work might be practised in Word and Sacrament as much as in the articulation of economic principles. I do think that the Report does a great service by thereby reminding everyone of the fact that in many senses, the Church is everywhere: in the actions and choices of individual members, in sector ministry and strategic representation to the world of work, in pressure groups and campaigns mobilising support for the low-paid, unemployed, and so on. The Working Party says, *'The churches have no special expertise to offer in the solution of economic problems'* (p. 177); but if we take all the contexts within which we might conceivably identify the presence and activity of 'the Church', then that does actually qualify as a heck of a lot of expertise! But at this level, what we understand to be 'Church' overlaps with 'secular' concerns, and its boundaries are permeable and forever shifting; but after all, I think that simply reflects the reality of 'Church', 'faith' and 'theology' anyway. And for that reason, I would refute the neo-Barthianism of Hauerwas and the post-modern Christendom of Milbank, simply because, as well as being insufficiently dialogical in theological terms, these models are sociological fictions and fantasies which bear no resemblance to the lived experience of Church and culture in Britain today.

So, although we are presented with a number of models of 'Church' within this Report, and of not one but many Christian experiences of involvement with the world, the Working Party does not properly address or engage with that diversity. As Malcolm says, *'... we are all dissenters these days*': but the problem, it seems to me, is that the question of denominational identity has been fudged, such that the Report inherits, by default, Church of England assumptions about how it speaks, for whom and from what position. Yet the Report fails to realise that all such theological statements are actually undergirded by practical ecclesial realities! The Working Party is keen to emphasise that '*The churches should have something to say which is different from the message of any political party or interest group*' (p. 176), and that the churches should be speaking with a distinctive voice: '*... we hope that this is not just another report about the economy which might just as well have been written by an economics institute*' (p. 176); but the insistence upon a discourse of speaking from general principles and values comes over as strangely disembodied and, despite those good intentions, rather unspecific. If it is theology in dialogue with economics and Church in conversation with policy makers, therefore, then I find it inadequately 'earthed' in everyday experience. In not wishing to privilege any one particular Christian denomination, the Working Party fails to speak from any clear tradition, grounded in the specific activities or practices of the churches.

Despite the Working Party's attempts to encompass social, racial and denominational representativeness, therefore, I feel that an opportunity to reflect the complexity and richness of ecumenism has been missed. I don't see much evidence of that diversity actually making any difference to the self-understanding of the Report, and in particular for a greater critical awareness of from whom it speaks, to whom and to what ends. In ecclesiological terms, these derive from different understandings of what it means to be Church, Body of Christ, People of God in both theological and sociological terms. That is, questions not just about the calling of the faithful into community as Christians understand it; but very real and strategic questions about how the Church as organisation and institution might intervene in the public domain to help attain a social vision of '*enough good work for everyone*'.[5]

REFERENCES

1   Archbishop's Commission on Urban Priority Areas, *Faith in the City*, London: Church House Publishing, 1985.

2   For some criticisms of the Church of England's pronouncements on social and economic issues, see Henry Clark, *The Church Under Thatcher*, London: SPCK, 1992: for subsequent theological reactions to *Faith in the City*, see Andrew Harvey, editor, *Theology in the City*, SPCK, 1989, and Peter Sedgwick, editor, *God in the City*, London: Mowbray, 1995.

3   R H Preston, *Religion and the Ambiguities of Capitalism*, London: SCM, 1991.

4   For further discussion of this, see: E L Graham, 'Theology in the City: Ten Years after Faith in the City' *Bulletin of the John Rylands Research Institute*, Vol. 78, No. 1, March 1996, 179-197.

5   *Unemployment and the Future of Work*, p.171.

Theological Comments on *Unemployment and the Future of Work*

Duncan B Forrester

Many of us, I suppose, were struck by the impoverishment of British political discourse revealed in the course of the recent election campaign. Politicians operated almost entirely in terms of slogans and soundbites. Issues believed to be sensitive or likely to worry or alienate any group of voters were sedulously sidelined and forgotten. Reforms and improvements were presented, as far as possible, as involving no cost. Apart from the Liberal Democrats, no one suggested increasing personal taxation in order to benefit the community. Issues like poverty, world development, disarmament and redistribution seemed to have disappeared from the agenda. There was precious little talk of visions of the future of British society, and hardly a suggestion that sacrifices now might be required from some for the sake of others, or now for the sake of a better future.

Two processes came together in that lacklustre election campaign. On the one hand, it demonstrated that Daniel Bell's '*End of Ideology*' had in fact arrived after many premature announcements. The collapse of the Marxist regimes of eastern Europe had left behind a profound distrust of ideology and grand overarching theories, partly for the very good reason that they are so effective at concealing what is really going on, disguising corruption and self-interest by '*the illusion that the system is in harmony with the human order and the order of the universe*' (Havel). For the moment, at least, nothing has taken the place of the old comprehensive ideologies, which for all their defects and problems were at least sometimes able to constrain selfishness and local political activity within a larger horizon than horsetrading. The other, more immediate, reason for the decay of political discourse in Britain was the desperation of the Labour Party to return to power. Ideological baggage that was uncongenial to middle England had to be jettisoned, and in the process much of the vision that had elicited the deepest commitment was also set aside. Lurking behind this is, of course, the deeper problem of how politics may be conducted in a radically secular society in which many people believe religious and theological views have no place or standing, while others fear that a society deprived of religion may quickly become inhumane and incoherent.

This is also the context within which we have to understand the strange renaissance of political religion in Britain, and the powerful phenomenon of conviction politics which emerged first with Mrs Thatcher, and is continued by Tony Blair in a rather different form. There are people around who claim that Christianity is true, and that it is necessary for healthy social life. We have today the resurgence of the Christian Socialist Movement, and that redoubtable Anglo-Catholic MP, Frank Field, arguing that the fundamental defect of the welfare settlement of the 1940s was that it was based on a simplistic and over-sunny account of human nature. A Christian understanding of human nature which takes both the *grandeur* and the *misère* of the human condition on board would provide, he suggests, a far better, because truer, basis for welfare provision and policy.

In this situation, the churches feel a special responsibility to contribute to public debate and to try simultaneously to enrich it theologically and to root it in the kind of realities which the Church, as people, knows at first hand. And the great British public looks to the churches and to theology with almost unprecedented expectancy to make constructive and significant contributions to public debate.

Two quite closely related, but distant, documents appeared during the election campaign as conscious attempts to influence the agenda and enrich the discourse of electioneering: the English Roman Catholic bishops' paper on *The Common Good*, and the CCBI Report of an Enquiry into *Unemployment and the Future of Work*. The first is purely Roman Catholic in provenance, but consciously addresses a far broader audience. It draws on a coherent body of social teaching which it believes to be public truth, capable of commending itself on strictly rational grounds to many who are not Catholics or Christians. The second is the distinguished and significant Report that we are discussing today, which is, of course, an ecumenical document which has its roots in a very much more complex, variegated and confusing tradition of social theology.

I want to undertake three things in this brief paper. First, to compare the two documents and ask some questions about magisterial Church interventions in political and economic matters in the light of recent US experience. Second, to enquire what *Unemployment and the Future of Work* has to tell us about the present state of ecumenical social ethics. Finally, to suggest that we still have some way to go before British theology can fully and effectively contribute to public debate, or the British churches relay marginal voices, particularly the voices of the poor and the unemployed, to the powerful.

The Common Good is a magisterial document in every sense of the term. It takes very seriously the calling of the bishops to teach in social matters as in doctrine and in personal ethics. It claims to draw on a coherent, incremental body of social teaching, believed to be accessible in principle to all, although the bishops clearly believe that the truth of social teaching is reinforced and exemplified in the Christian revelation. Drawing on this teaching the bishops none the less recognise limits to their competence. Most specific issues and political and economic choices have to be made by the responsible people within the authoritative horizon established by catholic social teaching. What the bishops offer is more a framework for moral/political discourse than an engagement with particular details of policy. They set out emphases, principles and directions, rather than specific policies.

If I am right that *The Common Good* essentially is offering a framework or method rather than policy conclusions, we can assess it in the light of recent similar moves in the United States. A number of prominent US Catholic theologians, most notably Dennis McCann, Richard Neuhaus and George Weigel, are proposing a natural law framework for American public discourse. Their position draws heavily on the work of John Courtney Murray, and is a response to a conviction that, in pluralist America today, political discourse is at the mercy both of special interests and of ideological distortion. McCann in particular seeks to provide ground rules for public discourse in the face of ideologies and interest groups which threaten to fragment the conversion, reducing it to mutually incomprehensible sloganising, or turning the discourse into a battle in which (in MacIntyre's phrase) politics becomes civil war carried on by other means.[1] Catholics should, McCann suggests, offer the natural law approach of Catholic social teaching as a structural resource for public debate and for adjudicating between the various interest groups' claims. The present fragmentation is acutely dangerous, these thinkers believe; theologians aware of this threat may act as *'facilitators who teach the rest of us the basic skills necessary for the intelligent use of the community's 'moral language'*[2] McCann, Weigel and others are deeply concerned at the danger of ideological domination of the public forum, so that the biggest battalions or those who shout loudest always win, and justice becomes (in Thrasymachus's phrase) the interest of the strongest; they believe a natural law framework - as in Catholic social teaching - might offset this danger by providing a resource for rational resolution of issues in the light of first principles. American society, Weigel and Neuhaus believe, is at a *'Catholic moment'* in which coherent ethical discourse, based on Catholic understandings of natural law, might give the Church a leading role in public moral discourse.

The situation they feel they are addressing is believed to be rather like G K Chesterton's parable about a controversy in the street concerning a lamp-post, which many people desired to pull down. A monk, personifying theology, is approached for advice and commences, in dry scholastic style, by saying, *'Let us first consider, my brethren, the value of light. If light be in itself good...'* At this point he is rudely knocked aside, a rush is made at the lamp-post, which is down in a moment, and the people *'go about congratulating each other on their unmedieval practicality'*. That is but the start of the trouble, for *'some people have pulled down the lamp-post because they wanted the electric light; some because they wanted old iron; some because they wanted darkness, because their deeds were evil. Some thought it not enough of a lamp-post, some too much; some acted because they wanted to smash municipal machinery; some because they wanted to smash something. And there is war in the night, no man knowing whom he strikes'*. So gradually they come round to the belief that the monk should have been heeded at the beginning. Only what might have been debated by gaslight must now be discussed in the dark.[3] McCann and his colleagues are like the monk, insisting that there should be a return to first principles. And they believe that there is such a depth of concern at the quality and the consequences of contemporary public debate that people might now be ready to hearken to the monk.

The process of discussion which led to the drafting of the US Catholic bishops' earlier pastoral letters on war and peace and on the economy[4] is suggested by McCann as a model of the kind of public discourse that he advocates, precisely because it allowed both the influential and the powerless to contribute to the discussion. For McCann, *'to keep everyone, including persons of influence, on board dialoguing, is deliberately to cultivate forms of solidarity and participation that could be just as much 'covenantal and eschatological' as they are truly Catholic.'*[5]

He is right to suggest that such dialogue is extremely rare. More usually: *'The influential talk among themselves, assuredly, observing carefully the protocols of well-insulated hierarchies and the marginalised share their egalitarian dreams, if at all, only in cries and whispers that even social activists have trouble deciphering.'*[6].

W D Lindsey, in a fascinating article, sees McCann's proposal as '*a strategy of management that will 'orchestrate' dissonant voices so that their unique tonalities will be muted and their specific textures suppressed*'.[7] The structure of the argument is disinterested and claims a kind of objectivity, but in fact it is intended to discipline all dissident voices, all positions which unashamedly claim to represent special interests, all other approaches which claim to be privileged. Both a 'preferential option for the poor' and a Niebuhrian understanding of the task as the balancing of our competing claims to reach a proximate and temporary settlement are excluded. McCann's position, claims Lindsey, is '*first and foremost managerial - a strategy for disciplining and silencing difficult Others.*'[8] The assumption that all positions are equally self-interested, and that Christianity comes in to provide a neutral framework within which competing claims may be adjusted, disguises a managerial strategy, a longing to be at the heart of things. As an old proverb runs - '*Every man for himself and God for all*' said the elephant as he danced among the chickens! The Church and theology appear as legislator and law enforcer, the body, like the MCC or the Royal and Ancient Golf Club, which makes the rules and the referee or umpire who enforces them. It does not have interests of its own, or so it pretends, nor does it promote the special interests of any group. Its task is emphatically not attending to, incorporating, privileging or responding to the voice of the disempowered, the voiceless, the Other. It regulates the game magisterially, with authority, from the heart of things not from the margins, arbitrating from on high on the ebb and flow of the disputes in the public square.

Protestants often look over the fence at Catholic Social Teaching with more than a little envy, for they have nothing quite as coherent and systematic to put in its place; and when the Protestant pastor stumbles into a dispute in the public square he or she is far less certain than the monk what is to be said. But is this really such a problematic stance? Perhaps we should learn from Foucault and other post-modernists that systematic discourse is often both exclusive and coercive. Perhaps the task today is not to present a sustained theory or a comprehensive account of the human condition, as much as to confess the faith in the public realm by offering 'theological fragments' of insight, in the hope that some of them may be recognised as true, and interest may be aroused as to the quarry from whence they came. And fragments, modestly presented, can indeed provide illumination in the public realm.[9]

Lindsey underlines the problem and the difficulty in attending to and incorporating and responding to the voice of the disempowered, the voiceless, the Other. These voices are conspicuously absent from most of our theologies, and only, I fear, heard rather *sotto voce* in *Unemployment and the Future of Work*, to which I now turn. This is unfortunate, for one of the main tasks of theology is surely to attend to and articulate the voice of the Other, to give them a hearing when so much else, particularly in academic life, conspires to deny them a voice. David Sheppard speaks of the Working Party hearing a '*cry of pain*' arising from '*a deep wound in the body, dividing those who are left out of decent opportunities from the favoured majority.*'[10] And the Report starts by reporting: '*From our year of visiting all the countries and regions of Britain and Ireland, north and south, we have returned shocked and saddened by the sharpness of contrast we have found everywhere between a favoured majority on the one hand and those on the other who are left out*'.[11] But the actual voice of the unemployed is rather rarely heard, and then only when the terms of the discussion have been clearly established, starting with general theological principles and then proceeding to careful social and economic analysis, in which the voice of the expert, the policy-maker and the academic come across loud and clear. For some of the members of the Enquiry, visiting areas of high unemployment and encountering the human reality of worklessness was '*a mind-changing experience*'.[12] To my mind the testimony of an unemployed man in South Wales reported on pages 41-42 is perhaps the most powerful passage in the whole report. More of this sort of material would have immeasurably strengthened *Unemployment and the Future of Work*, especially if it had been allowed to set the terms of the discussion.

The general style of the Report swings between that of a Royal Commission, and that of a book of theology - two powerful and effective forms of discourse, which are also discourses of the powerful, although here presented in a quite popular and accessible form. Yet it speaks to the head rather than the heart. I don't think it was calculated to promote empathy, to help us to feel that we belong together within the Body, to make us feel angry. I think I know why this was so. Confused, emotional, angry voices are disfranchised both by the rules of politics and by the rules of the academy. If you want to influence the government, you present a reasoned case, you don't burn buses or go on protest marches. But within the Church there is a dynamic which I would like to have seen figure more prominently in the Report, because it is an important gift to society. I have seen that dull, respectable, middle class body - a presbytery of the Church of Scotland - become angry as they listened to their fellow Christians from Urban Priority Areas speak about housing conditions, transport, health care, education, vandalism, and poverty in their parishes. And the presbytery's anger was a sign not only that they were listening but that they were sharing emotion, that they were feeling accountable to one another, responsible for one another, members of one another. And I have seen academics in theology almost physically draw back, their body language proclaiming this is no concern of ours when angry, muddled poor people interrupt serious, informed and well-intentioned debate about poverty and unemployment and homelessness, saying first of all, '*You don't know what you're talking about*'. And then they told their stories, usually in fragments, for as Rilke said, '*The story of shattered life can be told only in bits and pieces*'. It is a pity if the telling of these stories is left to the novelists (for Scotland one might instance James Kelman's *How Late It Was How Late* or Irving Welsh's *Trainspotting* as examples); for this surely is one of the tasks of theology and in particular of Church theology; allowing particularly the marginalised to tell their stories and relating them to the gospel story.

Unemployment and the Future of Work has moved beyond the older middle axiom approach to social theology in various ways. In particular, like *Faith in the City* and *The Church and the Bomb* it does not draw a sharp and impermeable curtain between middle axioms or principles and matters of application - specific policies and their implementation, considering the latter to be technical matters which can and should be left to the 'experts'. This is an important move for various reasons, two of which seem to me to be particularly important. The first is expressed particularly effectively by R H Tawney when he said, '*to state a principle without its application is irresponsible and unintelligible*'. The second is this: the press and indeed the general public read Church and other similar reports backwards. If the conclusions and recommendations are striking, distinctive, controversial and constructive they then read the rest to discover if these conclusions and recommendations come from an interesting source. Filing cabinets are full of Church reports that were arduously produced and raised not a ripple of interest because they were believed to be vacuous and overcautious. *Unemployment and the Future of Work* is not one of these. It will continue to be discussed seriously for a long time to come, and then will find its place in the history books. Its bold specificity is an important part of its value.

Unemployment and the Future of Work, if it does not highlight to any great extent experience, emotion and voices from the margin, does follow the older tradition of Christian social ethics by taking social science and 'the facts of the case', particularly as presented by the economists, with considerable seriousness. My secular social scientist friends who specialise in issues of work and unemployment think very highly of *Unemployment and the Future of Work*. They find its approach and its conclusions and recommendations congenial. But I do not get the impression that they feel that the theology of the Report is either particularly gripping or particularly illuminating.

Which brings me directly to the theology of *Unemployment and the Future of Work*. I am an advocate of Church theology, believing that theology is rooted in the community of faith rather than in the academy. There is theology, and Church theology, in the Report, particularly at the start, in the chapter on what the churches can do, and in the appendices. I like what I read. But it is not much, and if one compares the theology of the Report with its economics it is hard to conclude that the theology is as thorough, as serious, or as focused as the economics. It would be hard to argue that theology provides the framework for the document. This is, of course, more a criticism of the state of British social theology than of the theology of *Unemployment and the Future of Work*. It is sad that we seem to have made so little progress in social theology since *Faith in the City*. I hope other theologians will join me in saying *mea culpa!*

Unemployment and the Future of Work is an ecumenical report, by far the most significant such report since the British Council of Churches' work on Nuclear Warfare in the 1940s and 1950s. It is to be warmly welcomed as such. But it is a little disappointing that the ecumenical nature of the Enquiry does not seem to have opened up the broad range of neglected possibilities - perspectives from the rest of Europe, from the World Council of Churches, from Africa and Latin America - to enliven the still slightly cosy British scene: asking fundamental theological questions about the nature and the dangers of work, about our global responsibilities for one another and accountability to one another, about dignity, creativity and identity, about the power of the powerless and the privilege of the marginalised. Some of this is there in *Unemployment and the Future of Work*, sometimes in rather embryonic form. More would have been welcome. But what we have here is a distinguished contribution to public debate and to social theology, still rather Anglican in ethos, but worthy to be set alongside *Faith in the City* and *The Church and the Bomb* as major landmarks in the churches' exercise of their responsibility in and for British society today.

REFERENCES

1   Dennis McCann, *New Experiments in Democracy,* London: Sheed
     and Ward, 1987 and (with Charles R Strain, *Polity and Praxis: A
     Program for American Practical Theology,* Minneapolis: Winston,
     1985. My discussion draws heavily on W D Lindsey, 'Public
     Theology as Civil Discourse: What Are We Talking About?'
     Horizons, 19/1 (1992) 44-69.

2   McCann, *New Experiments,* p.96.

3   G K Chesterton, *Heretics,* London: Bodley Head, 1911, pp. 23-4

4   The later pastoral letters are much less interesting, both in terms of
     method and of content.

5   McCann, *New Experiments,* p.141.

6   McCann, *New Experiments,* p.142.

7   Lindsey, op.cit., p.51

8   Lindsey, op.cit., p.52

9   I have developed this in my *Christian Justice and Public Policy,*
     Cambridge: Cambridge University Press, 1997.

10   *Unemployment and the Future of Work,* p.v.

11   Ibid., p.1.

12   Ibid., p.54.

Is God Redundant?

Nigel Biggar

On most counts, the Council of Churches for Britain and Ireland has good reason to be pleased with its Report; and the rest of us have good reason to be grateful for it. *Unemployment and the Future of Work* is the most substantial Christian contribution to political debate in Britain since *Faith in the City* (1985). It (briefly) commanded the attention of most of the broadsheets, and even elicited their respect - albeit grudgingly in the case of *The Daily Telegraph*[1].

Economically, it makes a strong case for the creation of more paid work in service industries, both in the private sector by reducing the taxes and social security contributions borne by employers of low-paid labour, and in the public sector by general taxation; although it is not as thorough in meeting predictable right-wing objections as it should have been.

On the ethical front, its content is solid, even if the method by which it arrives at this is fashionably unmethodical. There are no obvious omissions in the set of social and moral principles it uses, and those that it does deploy are certainly Christian: a concept of human society as an organism whose members are mutually dependent; the consequent principle that economic inequality among us should not grow to the point where the majority prosper beyond the dreams of their grandparents while a minority still lack the means for a decent standard of living; and, perhaps most distinctively Christian of all, a compassionate regard for the poor.

Politically, economically, and ethically, then, *Unemployment and the Future of Work* has much to commend it. What more could one reasonably ask for?

There is something. *Unemployment and the Future of Work* represents the thinking of a body of Christian churches; so it is surely reasonable to expect it to have a strong theological dimension. I take it for granted that Christian churches have, as their specific responsibility, the task of declaring that committed belief in God, especially of the Christian kind, is vitally important for human flourishing, both in the next life and in this one. And I therefore also assume that they should be eager, especially in the face of modern and post-modern scepticism about Christian religion, to seize any appropriate opportunity to show or explain why this is so. If this task of theological declaration and explanation is not the defining responsibility of the Christian churches, then I do not know what, specifically, they exist to do; that is, I do not see what distinguishes them from any other social organisation with humanitarian intentions.

It is not that I think that Christian churches should always strive to be distinctive. Distinctiveness is not the point, authenticity is. But there will be occasions when, in order to be authentic, the churches must become distinctive. So, for example, relative to secularist humanitarians, they are bound to be distinctive in claiming that things like faith in God and hope for eternal life are important, even basic, elements of the human good. And relative to, say, Jewish or Muslim theists, they are bound to be distinctive in claiming that the compassion of God has taken the radical form of incarnate solidarity and of forgiveness instead of retributive punishment.

In the light of these assumptions about the specifically theological responsibility of Christian churches, *Unemployment and the Future of Work* is disappointing. It does, indeed, allude to the 'spiritual' or 'religious' dimension of the problem of unemployment. For example, it hints (in its Foreword) at the spiritual issues that lie behind social justice matters - '*despair, waste of God-given talents, contempt, hiding the eyes from the pain of brothers and sisters*' (p. v). But it does not pause to spell out what it means, and thereby to connect these 'spiritual' issues to 'religious' ones. Whose despair is being referred to? Presumably, the despair of the unemployed at their apparent social redundancy, their real social isolation, and their personal impotence. But what makes this spiritual, rather than just psychological? It is possible, but unlikely, that the Report was also referring to the despair of those who avert their eyes from the suffering of the unemployed, and even regard them with contempt, because, bereft of faith in God and hope for eternal life, they have come to see human life basically as a matter of what we can get away with - and that includes fending off, whether by neglect or by contempt, other people who make disturbing claims on our compassion and on our money.

A little later, *Unemployment and the Future of Work* mentions that the long-term implications of artificial intelligence raises some 'religious questions' about what it means to be human, and about how human work differs from the work we can get out of a machine, however intelligent (p. 15). But what, exactly, is 'religious' about these questions? Apparently, their answers: that human beings are made in the image of God and that, therefore, human beings (unlike machines) are capable of being genuinely creative. Obviously, the notion of humans as made in God's image is a theological notion; for it describes human being in relation to God. But in the Report the only element of its content that is actually referred to is anthropological; namely, human creativity. This is certainly a value that Christians should gladly affirm; and if any Christians doubt that, they could be instructively referred to the notion of being made in God's image as found both in the Bible and in subsequent Christian tradition. But it is by no means clear, especially to those outside of the Christian Church, why one needs to make mention of God at all in order to affirm the value of human creativity. Indeed, many would dispute the Report's assumption that this is a religious notion at all. But, beyond using the religious expression, the Report makes no attempt to explain or establish its theological content.

This is important because the concept of human being as made in God's image is one of the major anthropological principles of *Unemployment and the Future of Work*. Indeed, it is the first-mentioned of the several *'narratives and images of scripture'* that are said to govern its treatment of the issue of unemployment (p. 3). Since humans are made in God's image, they have *'the potential for creativity, responsibility and love'*, and for that reason they should never be treated as *'disposable, menial, and unwanted'* (p. 3). Society, in other words, has a moral duty to help the unemployed find ways of exercising and developing their God-given potential. All this is true and important and bears directly on the issue in hand. What more, then, should have been said?

Something should have been said to prevent the impression settling in the minds of non-religious readers that the notion of being made in God's image is a quaint religious expression for certain qualities of human being that all decent liberal folk take entirely for granted. Something should have been said to avoid confirming the widespread impression that when theology is not unintelligible, it is redundant. Because, when theology is unintelligible, then the Christian churches can at least strive to explain it; but when theology is redundant, then the sooner they volunteer to go out of business and stop confusing everyone by appearing to talk about one thing (God) when they really mean another (human being), the better.

So what might *Unemployment and the Future of Work* have said? It might have said that human creativity has significance only insofar as it occurs in the natural, given, created context of a set of moral values; for it is only

60

within such a moral 'horizon' that free, creative human choices can be regarded as valuable. Charles Taylor, the Canadian philosopher, puts the point nicely: *'Even the sense that the significance of my life comes from its being chosen ... depends on the understanding that independent of my will there is something noble, courageous, and hence significant in giving shape to my own life. There is a picture here of what human beings are like, placed between this option for self-creation, and easier modes of copping out, going with the flow, conforming with the masses, and so on, which picture is seen as true, discovered, not decided. Horizons are given.'*[2]

The value of human creativity, then, presupposes responsibility; and responsibility presupposes that there is something to be responsible to, which exists prior to one's decisions, and in that sense lies 'outside' of oneself. *Unemployment and the Future of Work* could have said something like this, and then proceeded to point out that part of the meaning of the (Christian) concept of God is that there exists a single, coherent, universal moral order to which human creatures are responsible. The biblical notion of being made in God's image places equal emphasis on creativity and responsibility.[3] We have the potential for creativity, but only within the given context of responsibility.

All this may be true, but how it is relevant to a discussion of the problem of unemployment? One way in which it becomes relevant, is through the problem of overwork: to be responsible *under* God means that one has a subordinate, and therefore limited, responsibility. A human individual is only responsible for doing the few things that he is called to do in his own time and place; it is his duty only *'to appear at once and well or badly to say his little piece as appointed'*[4]. The corollary of recognising human responsibility as the limited responsibility of creatures is the recollection that there is a divine Other who carries a greater, universal responsibility, and that the fulfilment of all responsible human work depends radically upon the work of God.

Faith in the providence of God, together with the correlative understanding of ourselves as creatures, then, is an important antidote to certain idolatrous kinds of overwork that are especially characteristic of secularist culture. This is overwork that is driven by a perception of humans as the sole bearers of (cosmic) responsibility, and therefore by a sense that our achievement and its preservation rest entirely on our own shoulders; which drivenness might be intensified by an anxious desire to secure a sort of *ersatz* immortality through the fame of our deeds.

The social significance of the institution of Sabbath-rest, therefore, should not be understood primarily in terms of recuperation from work or freedom for family and recreation. Primarily, Sabbath-rest is about the regular cessation of human work in order to acknowledge the fragility of its achievements and the dependence of its fate upon the providence of God. It is about the formation, through acts of worship, of a faithful spirituality; a correspondingly modest and resilient character; and therefore a regard for work that is relaxed in a humane, not a merely casual, fashion. Certainly, *Unemployment and the Future of Work* does not omit to mention the worship of God among the purposes of the Sabbath, but it places it last in a list of six; and it displays no understanding of its basic importance for spiritual and moral, and thereby social, formation.

What has the problem of overwork to do with the problem of unemployment? As the Report notes, there is evidence that some in Britain are doing too much work while others are doing too little or none at all. In addition to the task of work-creation, then, there is also the task of distributing more equitably such work as there is: '*It seems to us absurd, and also altogether unjust, that some people should be working so long and so hard, whilst other people have no paid work at all... Would it not be helpful if those who now overwork were to work less, creating more opportunities for others who now work too little or not at all?*' (p. 164).

The overwork of some is correlated to the un(der)employment of others; and some of the motives for overwork are rooted in a secularist spirituality, which is itself rooted in an atheistic metaphysics. Metaphysical beliefs do help to make certain ways of living seem reasonable, and metaphysical disbeliefs do help to subvert the purported reasonableness of other ways of living; and ways of living include ways of working. It is at this deeper, metaphysical level that I find *Unemployment and the Future of Work* wanting. It hints at the spiritual roots that feed the problem of unemployment, or our deliberate neglect of it. But it makes little or no attempt to use appropriate opportunities to uncover those roots and analyse them back to their religious source in disbelief or unbelief in God. That is, it fails to conduct a *theological* analysis and critique of the secularist culture in which unemployment is allowed to persist.

For this reason, while it recognises the need for '*a vital spiritual transformation*' (p. 7) of contemporary culture, so that taxes come to be regarded, not as a form of government extortion, but as fair contributions to the common good, *Unemployment and the Future of Work* assigns responsibility for this transformation largely to party political leaders (pp.101, 172). This is not inappropriate insofar as the task is to persuade the tax-paying electorate that an increase in rates of taxation in order to stimulate employment in public services will also benefit them by improving the services that they themselves use (pp. 98-9). But this education in enlightened selfishness hardly amounts to a '*vital spiritual transformation*'. That, presumably, would involve persuading comfortably-off earners and ambitious workaholics that, in order to give work to the un(der)employed, they should pay higher taxes and reduce their working hours even when it brings them no material benefit. It would be wonderful if party political leaders did lend themselves to such persuasion; but since it would involve recommending and justifying a theological vision of reality in which it makes sense not to view human life simply as a matter of what you can get away with, that task would seem to belong more naturally to the Christian churches and their theologians. *Unemployment and the Future of Work*, however, does not appear to recognise any special role for the churches in bringing about the necessary spiritual transformation.[5]

To summarise, in spite of its political, economic, and ethical strength, *Unemployment and the Future of Work* shows almost no sign of appreciating the churches' responsibility to read the social and economic situation in terms of Christian *theo*logy and *theo*logical anthropology, and to recommend this way of reading to a sceptical public. And because of the feebleness of its witness to God, its prophecy fails to penetrate deep enough beneath the surface of secularist culture to touch the spiritual and religious roots that help to nourish the problem of unemployment.

REFERENCES

1   For a fuller account of the Report's reception by the press, together with a summary of its main points, see my article, "Where There's a Will", in *Third Way* (May 1997).

2   Charles Taylor, *The Ethics of Authenticity,* Cambridge, Mass.: Harvard University Press, (1991), p.39.

3   One common, and perhaps the most textually apt, interpretation of the word 'image' as it appears in Genesis 1.25, is that it alludes to the 'images' of themselves that Ancient Near Eastern kings used to set up in outlying provinces in order to represent their authority. To be made in God's image, then, is to be made a representative of God's royal (governing) authority; that is, made to govern in his name and so *in subordination to* his will. This interpretation is confirmed by the second half of verse 26, where God authorises human beings to rule over other creatures: 'Let us make man in our image, ... *and let them rule...*'

4   Karl Barth, *Church Dogmatics,* ed. G W Bromiley & T F Torrance, vol. III: 'The Doctrine of Creation', pt. 4 (Edinburgh: T & T Clark, 1961), p.579.

5   To be fair, the Report does observe that support for a policy of employment-expansion paid for by higher taxes is especially high in the Christian churches, and it hopes that 'they can use their influence on public opinion as a whole to good effect' (p.172). But this still falls short of recognising the churches' responsibility to offer a *theological* critique of culture and a persuasive recommendation of a Christian *theological* vision of reality.